#WHATIS

#WHATIS
NUMEROLOGY?

SONIA DUCIE

This edition first published in the UK and USA 2016 by
Watkins, an imprint of Watkins Media Limited
19 Cecil Court
London WC2N 4EZ

enquiries@watkinspublishing.com

Design and typography copyright © Watkins Media Limited 2016

Text and photographs copyright © Sonia Ducie 2016

1 3 5 7 9 10 8 6 4 2

Typeset by Manisha Patel

Printed and bound in Germany

A CIP record for this book is available from the British Library

ISBN: 978-1-78028-953-3

www.watkinspublishing.com

CONTENTS

Why read this book?

My aim in writing this book is to provide beginners with an open, honest and accessible guide to the age-old subject of Numerology, showing how it can help you learn more about yourself and your true needs and how, with Numerology's aid, you can open up new perspectives that will help to transform every area of your life and the world around you.

Numerologists define Numerology as an ancient meta-physical science, founded on the cyclical relationships of sound and numbers, letters, the human personality and life events. You may think numbers are simply black and white digits that give us specific flat information, but they are much more than that. Numerology is an insightful way of working with numbers (specifically the numbers 1 to 9 as we will go on to see) that allows us to tap into their infinitely creative energies. Numerology, therefore, is able to reveal golden nuggets of information that can potentially change life on many levels – physically, mentally, emotionally and spiritually. When we start listening to what the numbers tell us, our awareness broadens and we are able to find our own natural rhythm in life, bringing out more of our true selves.

You may have read about Numerology in magazines or listened to friends discussing their numbers. However, you may not have realized how fundamental numbers are to existence. People often don't realize, for instance, how everything moves in numerical cycles from 1 to 9, which we can learn to interpret through our mind and intuition. I believe that, through Numerology, it is possible to gain enhanced clarity, truth, love, wisdom and understanding, therefore leading to greater fulfilment in our daily lives. So let the numbers guide you as they have guided many sages through the ages. You'll be amazed by the results.

20 reasons to start reading!

1 Understand the basics about Numerology
2 Recognize why certain numbers grab your attention
3 Discover how Numerology developed since ancient times
4 Utilize wisdom gained from names to enhance your life
5 Be more savvy about dates and how they influence life
6 Gain insight into behavioural patterns
7 Learn how to access hidden creative potential
8 Develop confidence by allowing yourself to really be yourself
9 Learn how to read people and situations more accurately
10 Feel more emotionally engaged with life
11 Explore strengths, weaknesses and potential in relationships, career, lifestyle and beyond
12 Learn to go more with the flow
13 Increase your ability to make decisions
14 Gain increased clarity and vision

15 Learn to trust yourself and life more

16 Develop your intuition

17 Better balance the inner, spiritual, and outer, material, aspects of life

18 Learn a new language that enables you to communicate with everyone in the world

19 Relate to the world and what is going on around you at a deeper level

20 Develop increased tolerance, compassion, love and understanding

Key features of this book

In the Introduction I explain how the whole of life is based on numbers, I talk about how I discovered Numerology, and why I'm passing my knowledge of it on to others.

Chapter 1 describes some of the key qualities associated with the numbers 1 to 9, explains where Numerology comes from and describes some of the main areas of life to which it can be applied. Chapter 2 explains how and why Numerology provides such valuable information and discusses more of its benefits. Chapter 3 explains what Personality Numbers are, why they are important, how to work them out and why they are a key to understanding why we act in the way we do. Chapter 4 looks at Life Purpose Numbers, explaining what they are, how they enable us to understand ourselves better and how they help to steer us in directions more in line with our deepest, truest needs and desires. Chapter 5 explains the significance of Soul Vibration Numbers and shows how, through them, Numerology can help us to probe into the deeper meaning of life. Chapter 6 examines Name Numbers and Karmic Key Numbers, which relate to personal goals and inherited qualities. Chapter 7 looks at General Dates and Personal Year Numbers and how they influence relationships, health, lifestyle, career and spiritual or inner growth. Finally, Chapter 8 covers Master Numbers and how they can help us collectively rise to greater levels of awareness. Finally, the 'What Next?' section at the end of the book explains how you can continue your investigations.

This book is designed to make Numerology as accessible as possible with the help of the following features:

- A Q&A approach that, chapter by chapter, explores the questions that are often asked about Numerology.
- 'Focus On' boxes that provide a deeper understanding of key terms and aspects.
- 'Try It' boxes that offer helpful tips on working out your numbers and interpreting what they mean.

INTRODUCTION

Why this subject?

Numbers are present in our daily lives in all kinds of ways, from telephone numbers, purchase order numbers and currencies, to wedding and graduation dates. When viewed through the lens of Numerology, all such numbers can open up a whole new world for us. They speak to our subconscious mind and bring to the surface infinite potential for change. They help us see through situations and tap into the innate wisdom within ourselves.

Numerology is a positive life force. It helps us to live in the present by providing solid, yet complete, awareness and insight. It enables us to reflect on the past and let things go. It helps us to change our perception and so to alter our future. In short, it can help us to make the most of life.

Numerology is based on the numbers 1 to 9, with zero representing the unseen, the energy behind the physical and the potential for the whole of creation. As well as having its own qualities, each number is constantly influenced by the numbers around it. For example, 8 is influenced by the numbers 7 (before) and 9 (after). Each is also indicative of the types of experience we have or may have in life. This is because each of the 9 numbers is associated with specific factors that can influence us at different physical, emotional, mental and spiritual levels (see page 24).

We are constantly influenced by the vibrational energy of numbers. By being more consciously aware of their essence, we can enhance their effect on our health and lifestyle, career and relationships, and more. Esoteric Numerology, the system I practise, creates the space we need within ourselves to connect with our inner self and so helps to speed up the process of self-transformation.

There is one more important point to explain. As you read this book, you will recognize some, but not all, of the interpretations I give. This is completely natural because we cannot see ourselves completely clearly. Having the courage to recognize the truth can be a real passport to change – to achieving success, happiness and inner freedom. So why Numerology? Because it really can provide you with all the answers you need to change life for the better.

Why me?

I discovered Numerology by accident. My father was a mathematician and from childhood I was fascinated by numbers. However, I did not realize there was an intuitive side to them until, when I was 32, a friend told me about her family's readings with Claudine Aegerter. I was so intrigued that I booked a reading with Claudine. As dramatic as it may seem, during that session I literally saw the light. I simply knew this was what I wanted to do for the rest of my life.

I suggested to Claudine she set up a formal organization, and the Connaissance School of Numerology was born. I trained with Claudine and have been a professional Numerologist ever since. I've now written 12 Numerology books, given countless radio, television and print interviews, run workshops, courses and business seminars, and have been teaching and training others.

This book is based on Esoteric Numerology, which is what I use to teach and train students. It encourages us to open our minds to intuition so we can contact our inner self or soul and see the bigger picture. Numerology provides us with lots of details. Esoteric Numerology gives us a fuller perspective on life and adds depth, so that we can see details clearly.

Over the years, Numerology has helped me to change from the inside out, both personally and professionally. It has enhanced my relationships and given me a new career. It has also stimulated my spiritual growth and really benefited my lifestyle. I am privileged to be teaching and working in the field I love and to be able to use my gifts to uplift others.

I hope that this book will be a springboard for readers to delve further into this life-changing subject. My hope is to show as many people as possible how they can benefit from Numerology and experience its power and influence.

Why now?

In an ever-more-hectic world, with longer working hours and so many aspects of life to deal with that can drain away energy, many people feel a need for something bigger and more meaningful to help ground them more into the present. Using Numerology to connect with the numbers that appear in all kinds of contexts in your life is one very effective way to plug in to the essence and recharge your batteries.

Numerology also enables you to identify your gifts, strengths and skills, and to feel more connected to life. It helps you to embrace life and feel more compassionate, tolerant and loving toward your friends, family and local community, thus having a positive knock-on effect on others, too.

Numerology is particularly popular during times of world transformation, which occur as a result of changes within the group consciousness of humanity, such as those that have been happening of late with economic crises, political instability and rapid technological change the world over. Like a best friend, Numerology can help to see you through both the good times and the dark times, providing a fast track for positive change. So I hope that you enjoy the exploration of this topic that follows and that you will benefit from the far-reaching power of numbers as much as I have.

CHAPTER 1

Where does Numerology
come from and how
does it work?

Like a computer ticking away in the background, numbers are doing a great job of regulating life at all levels. They provide a common thread that links the whole of life together, whoever we are, whatever we do, wherever we live. We can choose to notice numbers or not, but they are continually communicating messages to our subconscious mind and we act and react according to their influence. In this chapter we explore how Numerology developed and some basic concepts, so that you can start learning right away.

When and where did Numerology first emerge?

Everything was born out of numbers; since time began numerical cycles have underpinned and created the movement and expansion that have formed the universe. On earth we are obviously influenced by the solar and lunar cycles. We're also governed by seasonal cycles, the daily 24-hour cycle, the cycle of birth and death in nature, and so on. Cycles can be understood as numbers, patterns or rhythms that provide the foundation for existence.

Did ancient civilizations live according to Numerology?

Every generation lives according to cycles or numbers but ancient peoples applied Numerology in many different ways. Early man mainly worked with the numbers 1, 2 and 3. Number 3 is called the Trinity because there are often three different aspects to life, such as mental–emotional–physical, mother–father–child, sleeping–eating–reproduction, and so on. Ancient Egyptians revered the science of numerology and particularly the number 3, recognizing that numbers and life were full of energy in constant motion.

Which great thinkers have been Numerologists?

The Greek philosopher Pythagoras, who lived in the sixth century BCE, is one of the first individuals we can identify as a Numerologist. He seems to have believed it was for the esotericists of the world – who understood the journey of the soul (see overleaf) – to discover Numerology and use it wisely to guide humanity. Pythagoras taught that everything was born out of numerical relationships and, more importantly, it was up to the seekers to investigate these for themselves.

In more modern times the psychotherapist Carl Jung worked with the concept of 'soul' (important in Numerology), which relates to his work on the collective unconscious. Numerology brings to the surface hidden misunderstandings from the past so that they may be cleared and transformation can occur, which is what Jung's work was all about.

How has Numerology developed over the years?

Although Numerology has been around since ancient times, people's relationship with, and approach to, numbers has, inevitably, changed through the ages. Around the start of the 20th century, for example, many old systems (all systems are neutral) were re-written by numerologists in their own way to mirror the consciousness at the time and to accommodate the emerging needs of a new era.

Ultimately, it's up to us to forge our own understanding of life through numbers; our view of numbers will change a lot within the course of a lifetime. I know that when I began as a Numerologist at 32 I related to numbers differently to how I experience them now. For example, I associated the

FOCUS ON UNDERSTANDING 'SOUL'

In everyday life people often speak of 'body and soul', with many religions believing that individuals have a personal soul that continues to exist after their deaths. Numerology, however, often also uses the word 'soul' in a distinctive sense to describe our inner connection to the energy we are made up of, which also connects us to everyone else. Sometimes we may be watching something moving on the television news or gazing at a sunset and suddenly we are transported into another world; we can tangibly feel the connection to this 'soul' – like plugging into the source.

number 3 more with its fun, creative, outgoing behaviour and attention-seeking qualities, but now I identify the number 3 as more to do with the essence of being-ness, acceptance and divine intelligence.

Are there many different systems of Numerology?

Given that different cultures and individuals are always at different states of awareness or consciousness, it's important that there is a range of varying systems or approaches to accommodate everyone's needs. The most popular of these are as follows:

The term 'soul awareness', also important in Numerology, refers to realizing more and more that we are not separate individuals going about our daily lives. The more we become aware of this deeper connection, the more love and compassion we feel and give.

And the equally important term 'soul aspiration' describes our need to reach inward to connect with the overall group we belong to (humanity) – the hidden essence of goodness behind our physical forms. Living life consciously and 'soulfully' inspires us to do better, be better and to serve the greater good, all of which Numerology can help us to do.

Esoteric Numerology: focuses on the inner journey of the soul; relies on intuition to help us see the bigger picture in life. Origins: Ancient Syria.

Sacred Geometry: focuses on specific beautiful shapes in nature; each shape is considered sacred, is formed from precise mathematical proportions and represents its connection to the divine. Origins: Greece.

Divination or Prediction: focuses purely on nature or the outer world; seeks black and white answers to specific questions in order to ascertain the outcome before it happens. Origins: Ancient India, Tibet, China, Russia.

Gematria: focuses on the numerical value of words and phrases as they appear and are mirrored in life/nature, and on their connection to the divine. Origins: Ancient Babylonia/Israel.

Chinese Numerology: focuses on lucky combinations of even numbers (particularly 8) as they come in pairs. Origins: Ancient China.

Pythagorean Numerology: focuses on the numbers 1 to 9 as seeds for creation, with 10 a sacred number. Origins: Ancient Greece.

Vedic Numerology: focuses on the significance of past life karma and its resulting destiny, along with psychic interpretation. Origins: India.

Mayan Numerology: focuses on the 20 steps of awakening/ birth. Origins: Central America.

While each of these approaches has its own focus, it's reassuring to recognize that they also all share many qualities that are the same in essence. When I was working on the Numerology for hundreds of baby names from cultures around the globe for my *Choose the Perfect Baby Name* book I was amazed but not really surprised to see how the modern esoteric interpretation for each name nearly always matched the traditional cultural description given for it.

What numbers are used in Numerology?

While numbers such as your Personality Number, Life Purpose Number, Soul Vibration Number and the other significant 'Numbers' covered in this book (see pages 31–3 for more on these) are a great place to start your numerological explorations as they provide such a fantastic overview of many of the main aspects of life, other numbers such as your age, wedding date, graduation date, house number, school name and much more are all worth examining.

For all of the main number 'types' covered in Chapter 3 onward I will give starting point interpretations for each number from 1 to 9. Once you have figured out which of these single-digit numbers you need to work with in that area of your life, it's best to write it down and then spend a little time gazing at it in order to get a feel for it. Don't try too hard; the more you relax the easier the intuitive connection

FOCUS ON INTERPRETING THE NUMBERS 1 TO 9

As you will see later, the numbers 1 to 9 have different properties in different contexts but they have basic underlying qualities worth bearing in mind when interpreting general numbers, or a random number that keeps cropping up in different areas of your life.

1 Independence, unity, vitality, new beginnings

2 Balance, sharing, polarities, decisions

3 Creativity, action, reflection, expansion

4 Endurance, boundaries, structure, responsibility

5 Communication, perception, magnetism, change

6 Wholeness, community, kindness, completion

7 Sensitivity, patience, honesty, manifestation

8 Inner strength, re-evaluation, humility, revisiting

9 Wisdom, growth, power, transformation

will be for you to read its personal message. Alternatively, if a number jumps out at you from a street sign or an advert be open to this to see what messages it helps you to reveal using the general interpretations in the box opposite.

How do I work with numbers bigger than 9?

As the interpretations given in Chapter 3 onward are based on the numbers 1 to 9, any large number or multi-part number such as a date needs to be made into a single digit from 1 to 9 before it can be fully interpreted. These single digits are the most important numbers because they are condensed, potent and jam-packed with creative potential. Working out a number is simple, just a matter of adding together the component digits until they make a final single digit.

Let's look at some examples. Your Personality Number (much more about this in Chapter 3) is derived from the day of the month on which you were born. Someone who was born on the 17th (of any month) has a Personality Number of 8 because 1 + 7 (the digits making up '17') = 8. This person should therefore consider the interpretation for the number 8 in Chapter 3 (see pages 54–6). Another example: someone who was born on the 19th (of any month) has a Personality Number of 1 because 1 + 9 (the digits making up '19') = 10, and then 1 + 0 (the digits making up '10') = 1. This person can therefore read about number 1 in Chapter 3 (pages 44–5).

Larger numbers require more steps. For example, Apartment Number 2467 → 2 + 4 + 6 + 7 = 19 → 1 + 9 = 10 → 1 + 0 = 1. Apartment 2467 would therefore be a 1 in Numerology. However, you can also read about the numbers 2, 4, 6 and 7, which are sub-influences of the final overall number 1. They add flavour to the cooking. Remember to gaze at the numbers and your mind, instincts and intuition will do the rest.

Does Numerology apply to letters and words as well as numbers?

Like numbers, letters and words are simply sound vibrations at different frequencies. As such, Numerology can be applied to all letters in the alphabet. In fact, it is pretty simple to 'translate' words into numerical values – see opposite for the 'translation' chart.

Names in particular are often worthy of numerological study via the letters that make up the word. As well as your 'birth certificate' names, nicknames, religious names and many others are all worth consideration. See Chapter 6, pages 87–112, for much more on this.

If we apply this method to 'John Lennon', for example, we get the following calculation. The letter values for J O H N are 1 + 6 + 8 + 5 = 20 → 2 + 0 = 2 and for L E N N O N are 3 + 5 + 5 + 5 + 6 + 5 = 29 → 2 + 9 = 11 → 1 + 1 = 2. So in Numerology

both these names are a 2, adding to 4 overall. However, 11
(Lennon) is called a Master Number because the digit is
doubled – see Chapter 8, pages 131–7, for more information
on this topic.

In Summary

Now that we have explored some of the most fundamental
ways in which we can start working with the numbers that
underpin our lives in all kinds of respects, let's look in more
detail at the wide range of benefits of doing this and the
great value that Numerology can therefore bring to our lives.

CHAPTER 2

What are the benefits
of applying Numerology
in my life?

In this chapter we're going to look at the many benefits of Numerology before giving you an overview of the specific Numbers that you will learn how to work with on a practical level from Chapter 3 onward. We're going to explore some aspects of Birth Charts and how these can help us make the most of our gifts and creative potential. Even working with Numerology in a simple way can be life-changing.

What can Numerology be used for?

Numerology helps us relate to people and life in a more truthful way so we can be ourselves and really shine. It teaches us how to make good decisions, find soul purpose and direction, improve our behaviour, change our lifestyle and daily habits, address major life issues and understand health patterns. It also boosts our self-confidence, helps us change direction and brings us more into life so we can live more fully. Numerology is so practical and useful at times when we're moving home, changing jobs, finding our vocation, needing to develop our skills or for relationships and compatibility, and it brings clarity about the lessons we're learning and the timing of events. Numerology gives us all the information we need.

What is a Numerology Birth Chart and why is it useful?

A Birth Chart is your personal blueprint and a wonderful guide and support for you to live a better life. Birth Charts don't have any fixed format but instead can list many different 'Numbers' derived from all aspects of your life. Later chapters in this book discuss some of the most significant of these but we encounter or can calculate many more in everything we do – and include them in a full Birth Chart. Consciously working with gifts, qualities and challenges that become apparent in your own Birth Chart is awe-inspiring and insightful. You can see clearly what each area relates to and understand why you have been through situations in your life or feel like you do. If you are having issues with relationships, health, or anything else, you can look at the timing and your make-up and gain clarity to help you turn the situation around.

What numbers and words can help me the most?

As already discussed, numbers themselves and those derived from words appear in your life in all kinds of ways. However, I've chosen to focus on some specific 'Numbers' within the chapters that follow. These numbers provide a strong overall chart reading and enable you to gather together the most clarity about your behaviour, direction in life, soul purpose, inherited gifts, personal goals, family lessons, timing in general, and big issues. So let's look at the different areas of focus to see what they all relate to:

Personality Number (Chapter 3) – a key to show you how and why you act or react the way you do; defines personal characteristics, both strengths and weaknesses. Worked out from the day in the month you were born.

Life Purpose Number (or Life Path Number; Chapter 4) – a key to how you can strengthen yourself from within, revealing deeper 'soul aspirations'. Worked out by adding up your complete date of birth.

Soul Vibration Number (or Soul Number; Chapter 5) – a key to discovering more about the journey of the soul from the past (or past lives). Worked out by adding up the overall number from the vowels in your full birth names.

Name Numbers (Chapter 6) – a key to understanding more about your personal goals, desires, gifts, family issues, and so on. Worked out by adding up the overall number from a complete personal name, including first, middle or surnames, stage names, pseudenoms, and so on.

Karmic Key Number (Chapter 6) – a key to recognizing a skill, quality or talent inherited from the past. Worked out from your full birth name by converting it into numbers and then seeing which of the 9 numbers is/are missing.

General Date (Chapter 7) – a key to outer events, types of experiences, qualities, creative potential, soul growth and transformation. Worked out from any date.

Personal Year Number (Chapter 7) – a key to the temporary cycles that influence our health, career, relationships, spiritual and personal growth. Worked out from the date of your last birthday.

Master Number (Chapter 8) – a key to intuition, service and inner guidance for the soul, reflected in numbers such as 11, 22, 33 and so on that have repeated digits. These numbers can be found anywhere in your Birth Chart or General Date.

Can Numerology help me to understand myself better?

Numerology is like having a best friend or guide who knows you inside out. There's nowhere to hide because it brings to light more truth. Looking at yourself naked in the mirror through the power of numbers can sometimes be painful but the truth, once you see it, can also set you free. When you first open up to Numerology you may be stunned by just how much information it can offer you to help you become more self-aware, by bringing things to the surface to be recognized and transformed.

Can Numerology help me to make major life decisions?

Numerology can help you to make the best decisions possible as it can show you what's going on in the outside world, as well as connecting you to your soul within. Having this bird's eye view helps you to depersonalize situations so you can see life for what it is, not what you want it to be. This is especially useful with big life decisions such as whether to get married, have a baby, buy a house, and so on. The General

Date and Personal Year Numbers tell you more about why you might want to make decisions at certain times. They can help you ride the waves by informing you what each cycle is about so you can go with the natural flow of each number.

Can Numerology help me to choose the right career?

For some people choosing a career is obvious because if their parents were solicitors they simply follow suit (they share some of the same key numbers – genetic codes or genes). But it can be all too easy to rely on conditioning. By taking a deeper look at your key numbers introduced above, you may well get clearer insight into what career or vocation you would *actively* prefer to follow rather than doing what *others* want you to do. Alternatively, your numbers may simply make you more aware of the reasons for your current attitude toward your career. You may therefore decide to do something to transform your soul from within rather than change your job! Either way, your numbers will be encouraging you to tap into your own inner potential. It's all about using your gifts and skills and being yourself.

Can Numerology help to heal my relationships?

Although healing is taking place all the time spontaneously, you can also speed up the healing process by gaining a greater sense of self-awareness and connection to the world and those around you using Numerology. People get together for many different reasons: love, sex, friendship, companionship, work, having babies, emotional security, finding direction. Numerology can help to reveal the deeper purpose of all your relationships, understand the issues you are working on together, and shed light on why you were so attracted in the first place. By helping you see what lessons you are learning together it can really help you to relax, and enjoy and embrace your relationship more. It can also help to bring clarity and choice about whether to start, continue or end working, intimate, family or friendship relationships.

Can Numerology divine the future?

In certain parts of the world, such as India, Poland, Africa and China, predictive numerology or divination is very popular and it is generally very accurate because it is based upon statistics and thousands of years of observation. That is, if x happened previously, then y is likely to happen now, and z is likely to happen in the future. I have friends whose children, parents and all previous generations of their family have visited Numerologists to find out the overall 'plan' of their lives. Some of them tell me how they got married in the year that was predicted, moved countries when it was said, worked with certain skills as foretold, but they also tell me about things that didn't happen because of changes in the movement of the heavens.

Esoteric Numerology – the system I use – provides an accurate 'weather forecast'. That is to say it is correct at the time, but the conditions in the heavens may change. This makes you realize that you are responsible for your own journey. By connecting with soul you can make the most of your qualities, gifts and skills and embrace change. To do the best you can and be the best you can be within your set of circumstances is what you are aiming for.

Can Numerology offer wider insights?

As well as helping you to understand so much about yourself and others, Numerology can help you really feel the connection with your inner self or soul that belongs to the whole of humanity. Remember when you were watching the Olympics on television along with 1 billion other people on the planet and the buzz you got from the connection? It's a very warm, uplifting feeling as group or collective energy opens your heart, giving your life more depth and meaning. As Numerology is so unifying, it also reveals the many ways we can all co-operate to help heal the planet and to raise consciousness to that of love, light, service and wisdom.

Can absolutely anyone benefit from Numerology?

Numerology is free, and as numbers are around us all the time it can indeed be used by absolutely anyone, no matter what age, gender or background. Its benefits and results are profound. With a little key knowledge you can gain more clarity about important questions or issues in your life that may need exploring. Life communicates to us via numbers but it's up to us how we interpret the messages. The key ingredient is to trust our intuition and keep an open mind so as to enhance the connection.

Can anyone give a Numerology reading?

It's simple for anyone to use the information from Chapter 3 onward to give some amazing insights into either their own or a loved one's life. But if you agree to do a Numerology

FOCUS ON TRUSTING OUR INTUITION

Just as you relate differently to life when you're a toddler, child, teenager or mature adult, so too will the way you relate to numbers change as you grow. Similarly, as different cultures evolved through time, people started to relate to numbers in different ways. As we open our mind and become more aware of numbers in terms of how they instinctively feel to us in terms of their energy, it will take us to a whole new level of awareness and intuition, so do bear this in mind as you move through the chapters that follow.

reading for somebody else, just make sure you are doing it with their best interests in mind and not just to fulfil your own curiosity. Only ever give a reading for somebody who asks for one (resist interfering just because you want to fix things for someone). If you are quiet before you start interpreting things for them you're more likely to connect at a deeper soul level through intuition. It's really important to listen to their questions, to be sensitive, kind and compassionate, and remain non-judgemental. There are advantages and disadvantages in giving a reading for a personal contact. Some people feel it's easier to open up to those they know rather than consulting a stranger; others are more likely to guard intimate details from a friend and feel more comfortable visiting a professional.

When might it be better to visit a professional Numerologist?

While it can be really fulfilling to interpret numbers coming up in your own life or that of a loved one, if you are going through a serious crisis, need to make big life decisions or are feeling really lost, a professional Numerologist, who is so much more experienced in the numerological interpretations and who is also more detached from your situation, can be of enormous help. They can mirror back to you the important lessons and issues, and really home in on your situation so that you gain more clarity and the strength to do what you need to do next. It is reassuring to work with someone who can see the bigger picture and can empower you to take responsibility for your life.

What do I do once I've found a number to work with?

Once you have identified which of the numbers mentioned above you would like to work with first, the next step Is to know how to interpret it in order to apply it to your life. As explained earlier, in Chapter 3 onward you will see starting-point interpretations for numbers 1 to 9 within each of the 'Number' types covered. While the core interpretations of numbers are the same whatever system or method you use, the way I've written the descriptions in this book are from the way I see and experience numbers. It's essential for you to develop your own relationship with numbers – to arrive at your own conclusions, beliefs and interpretations based on experience, and to discover your own path in life.

In Summary

Now that we've seen just how far-reaching Numerology can be, we are going to explore the first numerological tool: the Personality Number, explaining how to work it out for yourself to gain insight into your core character and personality traits. This number can help you to understand your patterns of thought and behaviour, in particular any inherited from childhood conditioning, so that you can become more aware of them and change them if you choose.

CHAPTER 3

Can Numerology give insight into people's characters?

(Personality Number)

On the day you are born you take on an independent physical body and develop your own characteristics. The 'number' (between 1 and 9) derived from your day of birth is called the Personality Number and it gives you a lot of specific details about your desires, needs, behaviour and psychological make-up. For example, if you were born on the 8th of the month (any month), the qualities of status, authority and control will influence you. You may also be very stubborn and wilful, and want to do things your own way. See later in this chapter for more details on the qualities related to each of the numbers 1 to 9 in terms of this personality profile.

People who were born on the same day of any month share similar qualities. There are also, however, many other varying influences over the way they apply these qualities; family, friends, social groups, geographical location, culture, climate, the General Date and other numbers in their Birth Chart, past lives, and so on, so do be sure to take such factors into account. For example, if you were born in London in the 'Swinging 60s' (self-indulgence, sexuality, love) or in America in the 'Roaring 20s' (the earth and its abundance, deliverance) your characteristics will be tinged with that particular collective energy and this really makes a difference. Another example might be that if you spend a lot of time with certain people you start to take on their mannerisms too. This is fascinating because what you think of as 'my personality' is suddenly put into wider perspective, allowing you to see that we are all a part of a larger collective energy or group. Ultimately humanity is one soul.

Through awareness of your Personality Number you can start to let go of limiting mindsets. For example, if you have a Personality Number 6 (see pages 51–2) you may well cling to a need for beauty in physical form or perfection in your

TRYIT WORKING OUT YOUR PERSONALITY NUMBER

Your Personality Number is based on your day of birth.

The Personality Number gives insight into your behaviour, psychological make-up and childhood conditioning.

Example. If you were born on the 17th of the month (any month):

Add 1 + 7 = 8.

Your Personality Number is 8.

living space but 6 also contains the qualities of love and compassion, which can help you to let go of perfection and recognize what is really important in life.

Every number contains an abundance of characteristics to explore so that you can learn and grow. Behaviour isn't who you really are – the true you is your soul, full of goodness, love and connection. Instead, behaviour is a gift to show you how you can change things to become happier.

What qualities are associated with particular Personality Numbers?

Personality Number 1

Character Strengths. You're like a breath of fresh air – you breeze into any room and you light up the atmosphere instantly. You are full of vitality, enthusiasm and energy and give it out in all directions. You really catch people's eyes but inside you wonder what all the fuss is about because you're just being yourself. You are a natural leader who makes difficult tasks look easy and effortless. You plough through life by holding your vision in your mind and going for it full on.

You think strategically and are good at problem-solving because you have a creative mind. Original and innovative, you put people in front of new ways of working, living, or being. You're purposeful and direct, but are very accommodating when it comes to accepting others' opinions If you think they're right. You may work for little pay because it's the creative process that turns you on, but you are aware of this and are learning to ask for what you need.

Character Weaknesses. You dig your heels in and are too stubborn for your own good at times. You can hold on to ideas and goals for dear life, even when all possibilities are exhausted. Sometimes, though, you just put on a brave face and let others push you around and you can be a victim in life. You rely heavily on others for direction and can be dependent, but you're learning from experience that you truly only find purpose from within. By focusing your mind you jolt back to reality and move on.

Although you thrive off (mental) challenges, you hold yourself back from setting foot in new relationships, adopting a new routine or changing your outlook on life. You may want someone to dig you out of a hole but only you can do it – eventually you see the light.

Personality Number 2
Character Strengths. You are calm and placid, and at times when the world is up in arms you are there comforting everyone around you so that they feel loved and supported.

Support is a key word in your vocabulary. For example, you are constantly weighing up if you are either giving or getting enough support in your daily life. Ultimately, you are naturally open and receptive and you embrace life fully.

You long for emotional security and this is most important in relationships. You therefore work hard at creating a safe atmosphere in which you can nurture yourself and others. You may vet a potential partner cautiously, or the people who visit you at home, or who you work with, to make sure they fit your emotional template. You are good at feeling when it's exactly the right time to share yourself with others.

Character Weaknesses. You are a real pleaser and you love making people happy, but sometimes you venture out of your league all for nothing (you feel), which leads on to another issue. You are always measuring up how much love or money you have in relation to others. After a while you start to feel it's futile wasting time constantly making comparisons and getting emotional when you simply need to take responsibility for your own life experience, which is unique.

You can be highly protective of yourself because you fear getting hurt emotionally. The question is, do you notice your insensitive behaviour when you're in an emotional whirl? You're learning to become more aware of others' feelings.

Indeed, instead of lashing out defensively at those within your environment, you are learning to crawl into your cocoon where you can harmlessly centre yourself.

Personality Number 3

Character Strengths. You clown around and are happy to play the fool if it lifts people up out of their daily toil. You actively seek out fun and even on cloudy days you find something to laugh about. It's because of your optimistic, positive attitude and your happy-go-lucky nature that you do make the most of everyday life. You're very creative.

During times of reflection your mind is highly tuned to help you recognize truth and wisdom. You're adaptable and can change course at the drop of a hat should circumstances demand. You're confident and are prepared to try anything once. You can be highly flirtatious and affectionate – and you will do anything you can to help others.

Character Weaknesses. Your mind chatters and suddenly you find yourself lost in mental turmoil. Sometimes this leads to a complete scattering of energy – and even chaos – in your daily life. Perhaps you feel confused about which path to take because you can see so many options. You're teaching yourself to focus so that you can carry out one task at a time and harness your energy into the present moment.

You love talking, but sometimes you need to learn to be still and observe the situation so that you can do and say what's needed. Sometimes you can be highly critical of your own and others' actions and words, but you recognize that pattern. You can be easily distracted by gossip and trivia, to the extent that you block out what's going on around you. This behaviour can be a useful pressure valve at times, but real-time responsibilities do always call you back to daily life.

Personality Number 4

Character Strengths. You seek material security, yet you're willing to take risks. This is why you possess such interesting and diverse characteristics; one minute you're doing practical paperwork, the next you're off climbing Mount Everest. You have a passionate nature and although you seem predictable, you're simply not. You reach great heights in terms of success because of pure staying power. You have a total willingness to apply yourself to life and you thrive on responsibility.

You take life day by day, and for that reason you work through problems practically, a step at a time. You are methodical and are able to strip situations down to basics so that they become more manageable. You enforce boundaries around you so that you feel safe and also so that others can function practically and happily too.

Loyalty and friendship are very important to you; if a loved one lets you down you may cut them out of your life completely at the flick of a switch. At a later stage, when you've taken time out to reflect upon your behaviour, you will often instantly forgive and forget. Friends add to your security and you also put a lot of effort into being a good friend.

Character Weaknesses. You get bogged down over worries about everyday survival. Twenty years can slip by without you even noticing because you've got stuck in a rut. You keep focusing on bills, food and where you're going to sleep at night – the same old stuff. Practicalities are essential, but your emotional, mental and spiritual aspects need to be fed too. When you do emerge from your sleepy state you may take gigantic steps forward to change your life for the better. People may be dazed by the magnitude of the changes you make, which are often very dramatic indeed.

Life is not black and white but sometimes this outlook creates major issues and turmoil in your life. You will cling on to the most obvious solution even if it is not the best one in the long run, especially if you think it will save you time and money. But knee-jerk behaviour can send you back to the drawing board. At times you make dramas out of situations that aren't important, but perhaps you like that because it makes life more interesting. You can learn to embrace change.

Personality Number 5

Character Strengths. You are spontaneous and are likely to burst into a song or dance at any given minute wherever you are. Likewise, you may change relationships, career or home purely on a whim. 'The grass is greener on the other side,' you think. Luckily, once you fall in love with a project or person, you do commit through thick and thin.

You have an analytical brain like a computer, gathering information as it jumps from one program to the next. Your job is to pull all the parts together to find a way of merging the information into something that makes sense, and then to pass it on to others. You love making new connections. You're a natural networker who flies high on social media as much as in real life. You tend to say the right things at the right time and they make a big impact! Your mind is clear.

Character Weaknesses. Your zest for life leaves you feeling completely empty and void of connection at times. This is painful and can lead you to fill that empty space with addictions: sex, food, drugs, sugar, work, exercise. You may be drawn toward spirituality to help you feel connected to your soul and to enable you to connect more deeply with others. Utilizing your creativity can also help you to channel your energy into something that will lift you up and make you feel really alive.

You usually thrive off change, but walking a constant tightrope of not knowing – what life's about or what's around the corner – may leave you teetering on the edge. However, deep inside you do know when it's time to take yourself off for a rest or to meditate to still your mind, so that you can spring back to life.

Personality Number 6

Character Strengths. You function best in groups because they make you feel secure and safe, and provide a sense of continuity. You're enormously kind and open hearted and you make space for everyone. You're at home with small dinner parties as well as at business events for 500. You like to lose yourself in the group – if you're a musician then you love the overall sound the group makes, rather than just your own instrument (or the sound of your own voice).

You love luxury and sometimes you over-indulge, but you consider yourself a respectable human being and you want to be seen as a good citizen of the world. Respect is high on your list of priorities. You're learning to respect the choices other people make in life too.

Character Weaknesses. You become obsessed with things that aren't important. Through over-sensitivity you can allow a few spots on your face to ruin your whole day. But this teaches you to get life into perspective. Emotional insecurities plague you at times, but you're the only one who can change your behaviour by loving yourself and getting real about situations. Your saving grace is your keen interest in the outside world, which stops you focusing too much on yourself.

You would rather go without something than endure second best, including relationships – your perfectionist nature keeps life at bay. You know life can't always look or smell of roses, but take a look inside yourself and you'll find everything you need. You can be sensitive and fall into the rut of regretting things in the past. This is all so time-consuming; you eventually turn it around by grasping the lessons and lovingly move on.

Personality Number 7
Character Strengths. You're not 'built' to sit around day-dreaming; but you can be a bit of a loner, which gives you time to contemplate life and to think. You possess a powerful creative imagination and you're an amazing motivator and generator of productivity; one minute you have an idea and next minute it's done. You are challenging to keep up with because as soon as you finish one project you often hurry on to the next.

You see through people with your keen sense of observation and intuition, which unnerves you as much as anyone else.

Your insights are useful to help others see reality and they also help to keep you firmly anchored in the present. You are a no-messing, blunt kind of character and, although you believe in rainbows, life is often simply black or white. You have good manners and impeccable behaviour in company. You're incredibly patient with people too. Children love to be around you as you have an amazing imagination.

Character Weaknesses. You may be a little aloof, vague and detached from life and too much in your head rather than in your body. This may be because you feel hurt (or as a result of a situation from the past). You withdraw deep into your mind and heart for safety and protection. However, you naturally want to merge with others and you love being with people so periods of being 'out there' and within are natural.

You may be over-preoccupied with your health and sometimes display hypochondriac behaviour. Thank goodness you are able to see what's happening to you and pull yourself out of the quagmire. Otherwise life would feel heavy and draining on a day-to-day basis. A part of this issue may stem from your acute sense of self-centredness.

You can feel fearful of embarking on new projects or going out into the world. You're prone to panic and anxiety when life throws up obstacles and sometimes even when things go your way – especially if changes happen quickly. Sometimes you feel completely misunderstood, and your intentions are the opposite of what people think. But you are learning to let go of what people think of you, to walk your walk and trust the process.

Personality Number 8
Character Strengths. You project an air of authority, status and wealth, even when you're down to your last penny, because you're charismatic and powerful, certain and strong. You're also incredibly directional, which people like because they know exactly where they stand. You give others a sense of purpose. You love flattery and enjoy smooth talking, but underneath your shrewd nature means you know what's what.

Your goal is success and you want to be the best, yet you're always the first to empower others to do well – because you're humble. One of the ways you progress in life is by constantly re-evaluating. You're unafraid to address situations and get rid of all the dead wood. This process is then reflected in your outer daily life; you make changes in your relationships, career, lifestyle and so on. You're assertive and are keen to dive into new opportunities that will enhance material (or spiritual) growth. You also have an entrepreneurial streak.

Ambition and achievement go hand in hand for you, but sometimes you've noticed much can depend on being in the right place at the right time. You're cosmopolitan in your outlook and have sophisticated taste. You're super-organized, and will always want to direct energy into upgrading your experience of life.

Character Weaknesses. You have a big ego. At times you think you're so powerful you can actually bargain with fate. But then life deals you a tough hand and you have to cope with it by finding your backbone and taking responsibility like the rest of humanity. You may clash with those in authority, but you're learning that your way is not always the best way to achieve a goal.

You can be over-controlling, and surrendering can sometimes be your key to success. For example, your partner wants you to stop working late so that you can enjoy more quality time together. You may fear losing control because you know the power of your strength – but you can recognize the triggers. This helps you to lead a more peaceful life.

You have a fighting spirit, which is wonderful because it sees you through life-changing crises or tricky situations. But you can be aggressive, and bossy at times when gentle assertiveness can carry you further down the road and also win you friends along the way. You're recognizing that it's not up to you to shoulder the world and its problems because people need to work out issues for themselves. That creates win–win all round.

Personality Number 9

Character Strengths. You often appear larger than life and are very worldly. Indeed, you take pride in how much knowledge you have acquired and how much of it you can pass on to others. Your main theme in life is learning – books, courses, conversations, webinars, relationships, personal development – you name it, you've tried it. Self-improvement is all-important and so is education because it broadens your horizons. You love travelling to new destinations on educational missions, humanitarian or charitable work, or to work on environmental projects. The bigger picture concerns you to the extent that you may become an avid campaigner for everything from animal welfare to human rights. Again it's about passing on knowledge and helping others.

You possess an unshockable 'I've seen it all, done it all' attitude to life and are liberated and broadminded. But you have a sensible side and are incredibly grounded in real life. Hard work is natural to you – you just see what needs to be done and get on with it. You're kind, tolerant and understanding. You set the bar high and can be an idealist

– you pressurize yourself to get things right. You are able to see the very best in others. You're patient beyond belief and never give up on people who need help. You love giving.

Character Weaknesses. You possess a rebellious streak and can be all fire and passion, which is powerful behaviour. You don't take no for an answer because there are no boundaries to stop you achieving your goals – knowledge and wisdom. You think you can change the world but naivety provides you with big lessons in life. You can, however, be the spark to the flame that lights others' torches and in a group you can make all the difference.

You sometimes project an air of superiority, which turns people off because they want you to be your true self. That said, humour is your saving grace and you're happy to make a fool of yourself to uplift others.

You want to do the right thing but you have a critical mind and you're quick to judge, which gives you 'headaches'. Then you remember that what's right is different for everyone and let go of labelling people or situations. Sometimes you suddenly act 'out of character', just to experience a different way of life. You can protest about your surroundings, but you really are like a chameleon, adapting graciously to your environment, and making the best out of every day.

CHAPTER 4

Can Numerology influence my soul aspirations in life?

(Life Purpose Number)

When you add up all the digits in your full date of birth you arrive at your Life Purpose (or Life Path) Number, which influences your deeper soul aspiration. This calculation involves you first taking your day of birth (personality, behaviour), then your month of birth (broadening horizons), then your year of birth (group energy) until finally you arrive at your destination – your Life Purpose Number. So you start off learning about your external character and eventually you are able to go within to tap into the collective creative energy of soul. It's great to have teachers, or friends and family, who help give you a sense of direction in life, but true purpose can only come from within.

Early on in life it is normal to be preoccupied with building your own 'castle', relationships, career or lifestyle. But when you mature in age, or even spiritually, you often start to want to do what's best for the group, learning to put others first. Your Life Purpose Number can help you behind the scenes to keep your life on track in this sense.

What qualities are associated with particular Life Purpose Numbers?

Life Purpose 1
Your path is to find courage within yourself to do the work you need to do in life. For example, it takes courage to look at

TRY IT WORKING OUT YOUR LIFE PURPOSE NUMBER

The Life Purpose Number is based on your full date of birth.

The Life Purpose Number influences your deeper aspirations and the inner journey of your soul. It gives you direction in life.

Example. If you were born on 14.11.1974:

Add $14 + 11 + 1 + 9 + 7 + 4 = 46 \rightarrow 4 + 6 = 10 \rightarrow 1 + 0 = 1$

Your Life Purpose Number is 1.

Note for throughout the book that in calculations with day and month numbers you always consider them as whole numbers first. In the example, 14.11.1974, add $14 + 11$ and not $5 (1 + 4) + 2 (1 + 1)$ This is because the Day or Personality Number 14 has 13 numbers within its sphere, and the month number 11 has 10 numbers contained within it. The year number is always added up as single digits as it is a long number.

your mistakes and be prepared to change. It takes courage to be your true self rather than the person everyone else wants you to be. And it takes even greater courage to keep going at times when there seems no particular purpose to do so at all. You're ace at inspiring courage in others though.

Life Purpose 1 brings independence, an ability to set a new vision and a willingness to take responsibility for your mind, body and spirit. You may fear getting hurt in a relationship even though you appear strong on the surface. Perhaps you're always telling friends, 'I don't need anybody,' but this is an empty pretence. Your soul aspiration is to learn to listen to your inner self and to follow your inner spiritual focus and drive and, when you do, you'll become a natural leader.

Life Purpose 2
Your soul needs to relate to people at a deeper level. You actively seek out work collaborations, a soul-mate, and people you can hold hands with as you journey through life. Paradoxically, sharing may not feel natural, but you learn to accept that two pairs of hands can make life easier. You discover the power of co-operation and harmony.

There is always duality in life – day and night, dark and light, cold and hot. Likewise your soul bonds with your personality and they lovingly learn to work things out together. Sometimes the personality is in charge and your desires overtake your existence; at other times your soul leads and your desires simply melt away.

Compromise is often frowned upon as a sign of weakness. But it takes incredible inner soul vision and sensitivity to be able to see a situation from both sides and then to reach a mutual agreement. Your soul is filled with wisdom learned from past experiences; you aspire to let love and inner wisdom blossom and grow and to bring love to the world.

Life Purpose 3

Happiness can breed spiritual inertia, because often when you're merrily pedalling along in life, cocooned in your own little bubble, you're not going to want to stop and examine how you can make life better for others. Hence, uncertainty and instability can be productive from a soul perspective as they can help you to look at what's really going on and move on.

The aspiration of Life Purpose 3 is to be able to recognize the greater plan as opposed to lots of little plans. Your aim is to become prolifically creative. You may be a great artist, writer, entertainer, sportsperson, or work with your hands. You really need to express the feelings and gifts that you have inside; others are inspired by your creative flair and capabilities.

Your mind is a powerful tool because it sees through everything – it's certainly not taken in by material life or by the emotions. Your soul aspires to explore mind (and the way people think) so that it can be used to expand people's vision and create more acceptance of life as it is.

Life Purpose 4

You aspire to bring order out of chaos, and this process gives you many important lessons about responsibility. You're likely to take on big projects in terms of soul growth and you opt for as much growth as is possible in a lifetime. You love routine and structure, but you still willingly dive into the great unknown and allow a new regime, a better way of living, to take over. With soul in charge you know that sometimes structures need to crumble and be rebuilt. If you look back at life when you were young, for example, you can truly see that life and consciousness were radically different then to how they are now. You know you need to grow up and to become a fully functioning adult soul, a shining light in life, in order to be able to make a real difference.

You're passionate about change and embrace hard work, so you get incredibly irritated by 'slackers' (perhaps they've earned a rest). You can be impatient for change but this only compounds your frustration about life. You can also get annoyed if you don't get exactly what you want. But give up, give in, and give over because your soul is ultimately in charge and knows what's for your very best. Change starts with one step, but it's your soul quality of endurance that keeps you going on and on. There's always more work to do.

Life Purpose 5

You aspire toward freedom – freedom of speech, freedom of movement, freedom to experiment in life – so that your soul can grow. You may be a homebody who lives in the same house all your life, which makes you feel secure, but there's a big wide world out there waiting to be explored. 5 is the number for the mind, which is always free to explore without prejudice. Indeed, you may have an illuminating mind that truly sparkles and magnetizes people to you, and you share your knowledge and emotional intelligence with others.

Sometimes you become mentally fragile (too much energy trying to get through your system at the same time) and you become overloaded with information. Through awareness you will know when it's time to slow things down so that you come back to yourself, or when you need to accelerate and start running with the wind.

Common sense and acute perception help you to separate fact from fiction so you can make intelligent decisions. You certainly embrace change. You're incredibly sensitive underneath the cool, magnetic and charming exterior and you aspire to clear out emotional debris hidden in your 'cupboards' and to bring soul into life.

Life Purpose 6

Your soul aspiration is service. Service sometimes requires you to give up your personal needs to provide for the group. For example, you may choose to take on a colleague's workload because he needs to get away early. Service can be as simple as offering a smile instead of being miserable, because your moods influence others in a powerful way.

A big part of your soul work (your deeper connection to life) is to work through the glamour of your emotions, which can colour situations and give you mixed messages. For example, you may feel that your partner doesn't love you (enough) but this is simply how you feel and the reality may be 100 per cent opposite. You feel life so deeply and sometimes take people's comments to heart. But reality is the best comfort blanket that brings you back to your senses.

Your inner wisdom helps you to grasp hold of situations by relating them to the bigger picture, so you can see what's important. You aspire to make good choices that will benefit the group. Ultimately you feel at your happiest when you know everyone else is happy and getting their needs met too.

Life Purpose 7

You often feel as though you are invisible – people literally overlook your needs, forget you're in the room and at times blank out your very existence. This is because you're so good at keeping life running smoothly and materializing magic for others that they only really notice you when it all stops. However, you are able to reach the stars through inner reflection and soul awareness, and you soon realize how incredibly lucky you are for life to provide you with opportunities to shine. Your soul is teaching you to love invisibility and embrace the process of manifestation, which is a natural process.

You aspire to speak the truth when it's for the highest good. This is challenging at times when you know it can change a situation dramatically or alter life forever. You can be blunt on occasion – people like you to point out things that need addressing. Sometimes people find your directness tough, because they don't want to look at the issues or are running away from facts.

You are intuitive and are learning to trust yourself and your inner guide (your soul). You are incredibly aware of life and spirituality, and you feel at one with nature. You may be ambivalent about your sexuality because soul is genderless and hermaphrodite (male and female energies constantly fuse together as one). Your Life Purpose is to trust life so that your true self can really dazzle and shine through.

Life Purpose 8

You can be a tower of strength to others and you're empowering to be around. Of course you realize that you cannot solve people's problems or make them strong: they need to do this for themselves. But you do offer them practical direction. You may explain how certain meditation techniques or a change of diet have helped to improve your quality of life. But it's up to them to bite the carrot (or not), and they'll only do so if it's what they truly need.

You aspire to rid yourself of outer illusions – you're in real life so wake up. This is easier said than done because as soon as you've cracked one level of an issue, another layer mysteriously appears. But this keeps you motivated, and spiritual will drives you along. You may love and even seek out obstacles purely because they can teach you how to overcome the impossible. At times you do hit a brick wall, but this drives you to internalize (to connect within) in order to dissolve inner roadblocks and to find strength.

You know there is a higher power governing the whole of life and you aspire to follow the highest spiritual principles possible. You are very obedient. For example, if life throws you a difficult lesson you do not fuss and fight – playing your will off against the will of the divine – you simply surrender with humility and take the lesson as a gift. That is real success. You may possess business flair and that brings many lessons around responsibility too.

Life Purpose 9

Your soul aspires to gain wisdom through your experiences in life. The wisdom stores up so that it can be accessed at a moment's notice when somebody needs your help. Your soul is only truly fulfilled when you're giving to others and doing your very best in life. You can be genuinely selfless at times and you may carry out tasks for no personal gain whatsoever. You lead by example and you're very practical.

You have a way of expressing yourself creatively that uplifts and inspires others because your soul has an incredibly expansive view of life. You see the world and all its people as one and are passionate about inclusiveness and equality. You will fight to protect the underdog, because you know we've all been there, and they deserve your empathy. You are incredibly generous with your time and money and are prepared to give away your last penny to a charity or cause even if you've got nothing left yourself. You see the highest possible potential in others yet you don't interfere – live and let live.

CHAPTER 5

Can Numerology help
me find the deeper
meaning of my life?

(Soul Vibration Number)

When you add up the number values from all the vowels in your full birth name you arrive at your Soul Vibration (or Soul) Number, which will give you insight into the experiences your soul has been through in the past. Soul is the invisible energy that bonds together the spiritual and material aspects of life. Soul is immortal and contains the essence of the lessons we've learned throughout many lifetimes. Soul is wise because it has learned the hard way through human suffering, joy, and the aspiration to grow. Growth requires input, and that's where our Soul Vibration Number can help us by showing us what our deepest inner yearnings are and guiding us to use this wisdom well.

When we look at a person we cannot see the journey of their soul or past lives on the surface. We can only see within ourselves and recognize what vibrations we have brought with us from the past. The Soul Vibration Number can help us to feel connected to humanity and be more in touch with real life.

What qualities are associated with particular Soul Vibration Numbers?

Soul Vibration 1
Your soul yearns for one-ness and unity. You feel the inner connection to the light, to where you've come from, and now

TRYIT WORKING OUT YOUR SOUL VIBRATION NUMBER

The Soul Vibration Number is based upon the vowels in the full names on your birth certificate. (Vowel values are listed above, in the box on page 27. Don't forget that the letter Y is classed as a vowel for Numerology purposes.)

The Soul Vibration Number highlights wisdom acquired from past (life) experience and also the deeper yearnings of your soul.

Example. Samantha Clare North:

Samantha A(1) + A(1) + A(1) = 3

Clare A(1) + E(5) = 6

North O(6) = 6

TOTAL: 3 + 6 + 6 = 15 → 1 + 5 = 6

Samantha's Soul Vibration Number is 6.

you are set on using this abundantly creative energy. You may be an ideas person, able to provide soul vision to others, or you may be an inventor. Sometimes you think that the world revolves around you until you remember the one-ness again. This realization frees you up and injects you with vitality and energy so that you carry on with your creative vision.

You can be naive and very playful, with an innocent sense of humour. Sometimes you're so busy focusing on your inner vision that you don't even notice that you are being misguided. Although tunnel vision is wonderful at those times when you need to accomplish an important task! But use your willpower, be more assertive, and don't allow others to slow you down or pull you off course.

Your soul is full of pure intent, which people do not always recognize, particularly if they have a constricted outlook on life. While you don't play victim, it's important to become aware of the impact you're making on other people's lives.

Now it's time for breaththroughs – you can do it! You can take responsibility for your creative mind and take those first steps along a new path as you hold a new vision for the future. Finding your sense of direction can be challenging if you don't identify with the new energy that's permeating your soul and you may not know how to apply it to life. However, that is all part of the wonder and awe of the journey. Every day there is something new to learn; every day there are new people to meet, and the possibilities of new inner discoveries.

Soul Vibration 2

Your soul yearns for love. The world is packed with love but if you can't feel it then life becomes a vacant universe. To feel love you need to be receptive and be able to remove the layers of resistance that you create for yourself. If you've been burned in a relationship, for example, you may feel too sensitive and vulnerable to allow yourself to got involved with a partner for a long time. By connecting with the love within your soul and learning to love your true self, you can allow yourself to form close associations and be loved by others.

When love is your driving force anything is possible. You can overcome little insecurities about who or what you think you are and give over to the greater energy of love. Love doesn't always mean getting what you want; it also means being able to love the soul of a person and see the reason why they are (acting) the way they are. When you see people with the unconditional love of the soul it is very freeing.

In the past (or past lives) you may have been cold toward people. You may have felt that people didn't like or love you or felt your love was unwanted. Perhaps you couldn't see other people's points of view and even when you did you exerted strong emotions to stamp out the feelings. Now it's time for your soul to use the power of compromise. Your soul can be considerate toward others' feelings and you can put others first. Indeed, your soul is so sensitive that you can intuitively pick up on what's needed in all situations and then offer help with kindness and consideration.

Soul Vibration 3

Your soul yearns to express itself in as many different ways as possible, by creating, doing or simply by being. Your very presence (the presence of your soul) may be enough to comfort somebody who is sick or provide (you or them) with strength during difficult times. Sometimes there are no words to say but it is enough to feel the connection of the energy between you. Have you noticed that some people say little yet you can tangibly feel their powerful presence?

Self-expression comes in many forms. Perhaps you're great at communicating, writing or baking cakes. You may love painting and artwork, which helps you to express the depth of your soul. Soul expression is so important that you can easily feel frustrated if you are unable to get out what's inside. At times your energy can be like a dam holding back a flood that builds up and eventually breaks in resentment, but you recognize this and aim to express yourself fully.

In the past (or past lives) you may have been highly critical of others' imperfections and your own. You may have felt confused, disoriented or unstable. You did not know how to express yourself or how to break free from troubling issues within yourself. You may have been unable to do what was needed or suffered from mental exhaustion from over-worrying. Now you can reflect upon life regularly so that you can see what needs to be done and let go of superfluous requirements. Life is on the move and you keep adapting, changing and growing according to your environment. Your soul feels the joy within and you consider yourself lucky; life is the blessing and you make the most of every single day.

Soul Vibration 4

Your soul yearns for responsibility. Responsibilities are the key to growth. You're a plodder but sure-footed – your soul works hard to create a strong foundation. You know you need to walk before you can run. When your mind is focused on the work at hand you can become a high achiever.

Your soul builds a strong empire. You explore the physical, emotional and intellectual landscapes within yourself, and also outwardly in the world – because these are your tools for survival. Survival of soul is inevitable, but the survival of your personality is fragile. At times you may be too attached to life being exactly the way you want and you organize others in a masterly way to fit your plans – they may have little choice. However, your soul is willing to give up your attachments at a moment's notice because ultimately it's your inner self, your soul, that provides you with the next step.

In the past (or past lives) you may have been involved in various conflicts with others – or within yourself, as your soul and personality were in battle to see which side would win. What you want and what is best for you to do are two completely different things; the work of your soul is to bring them together. Perhaps, for example, you were very hesitant and disorganized, which was counter-productive to your normal practical approach to life. By internalizing and connecting with your soul you were able to find out what lay lurking beneath the disorganization and in doing so took full responsibility to get yourself back on track.

Soul Vibration 5

Your soul yearns for change. Life is change, so there is plenty of room for your soul to grow. You may seek out adventures by travelling the world, learning a new language, and so on. But the greatest adventure of all is to dive within your mind and soul where there are endless realms to explore, and this promises to keep you busy. Change brings new sets of circumstances and different perspectives. Soul provides you with great mental agility in order to process the speed at which life moves, which is very helpful as your mood, outlook and situations change regularly.

Life is in a constant state of movement, and the only stillness you can find is within. Your inquisitive mind is always seeking explanations in life. You may be an avid reader, researcher or communicator, and this constant absorption of new information helps to speed up the process of change. Most of the time you manage to stay on top of the whirlwind of life but sometimes you become overloaded by mental stimulus and 'too much information'. You can be preoccupied with passing on your knowledge, but the world will not stop if you stay quiet for a while. At these times soul helps you to make sense of life by providing you with inner guidance.

In the past (or past lives) you may have escaped into the recesses of your mind in order to avoid facing challenges. Perhaps you led a monotonous existence. You may have been difficult to pin down as you were always changing your mind about commitments. At times you were focused on getting a quick thrill – intellectually or physically – to stimulate excitement, experience and growth. However, you know that real change takes time and provoking artificial situations can backfire. Your inner self provides you with real substance to be able to grow as a soul from the core. You realize that your grounding fork is within.

Soul Vibration 6

Your soul yearns for justice. The scales of justice can be heavily laden with emotions and it saddens you when situations are read out of context. But life changes – one minute you're looking at a situation one way, then it suddenly flips 180 degrees and you see it completely differently. You have the choice – you can take on the expansive view of your soul, or see life from the narrow view of your personality.

You are fair on yourself and others. You are able to internalize and make contact with your inner wisdom, which gives you a deeper view of life. You may not always like what you need to do, but if it's for the benefit and growth of the group, then you will do what's best. Soul is not punishing you for being less than perfect or for the choices you make in life. Sometimes you dig in so deep that you lose sight of the objective, which is wholeness. Your soul is growing all the time and gaining wisdom from every single lesson learned. It is an ongoing process of love, light and life.

In the past (or past lives) you may have been very obliging and been used or abused by others. You may have been discontented with everyday life and unable to commit in relationships. Perhaps you were self-indulgent emotionally and manipulated situations to get your own way. You may have found it hard to master your instincts sexually and perhaps you were a predator, satisfying your personal or sexual needs to the exclusion of everyone else's. Now you do respect others completely, because you respect yourself. You love people and life and want to preserve that status. You also focus on putting others first, which is a complete turnaround. Indeed, you are careful not to impose your needs upon others and only walk through a door when you are invited. Soul welcomes you in.

Soul Vibration 7

Your soul yearns for transparency. You are highly emotional, highly spiritual and can tune in to the higher vibrations of the soul. As a result of your refined sensitivity you find it extremely challenging to be around people who are evasive, illicit or dishonest in any way. Even to the extent that, if you discover someone has told 'white lies', it will ruffle your feathers enough to drop them like a hot potato and likely never go near them again. But even you tell white lies at times.

When you suddenly become angry or sad you know you are reacting to the energy or quality of someone or something in front of you that's reminding you of the past – everyone has these moments. You may have keen interests in philosophy, psychology or spirituality, so you will naturally analyse situations or even dissect them to get a good look. However, the easiest way to remove trauma, stress and anxiety is for you to reflect within, to connect with your soul so the greater energy of good can illuminate truth in any situation. Introspection is natural with Soul Vibration 7, but it takes time to be willing to see truth and to take responsibility for life.

In the past (or past lives) you may have suffered from spiritual pride, perhaps feeling you were at a higher level of vibration than somebody else. You may have misinterpreted facts or rejected others' truths. You may have tried to force a square peg into a round hole and wondered why people don't feel they can fit in with your life, or vice versa. At times you may also have taken life too personally. But life is a healing process; if you apply soulful mindfulness to your everyday life it will get easier. You can also intensify your spiritual growth by becoming more aware of others, and by listening to the inner messages from your soul.

Soul Vibration 8

Your soul longs to wake up spiritually, and you know that when you apply your mind and soul great things are possible. You're conscientious and organized, and you approach goals with vigour. You may not always recognize spirituality (higher truth) within yourself but your ability to connect deeply with the purpose of life (love, spiritual growth, oneness) means you are already aware of it. Getting on with life and being grounded (with the soul as the anchor) is your gift.

You're incredibly talented at carrying the can for others – responsibilities bounce off you and you handle them many at a time. And when you're taking responsibility, you can empower others to do the work they need to at a soul level. You are bold and shrewd when it comes to the practical and material life, but beyond your tough exterior your soul has taught you how to soften your approach through humility.

In the past (or past lives) you loved flattery and you avidly searched outside yourself for personal recognition. You wanted to prove to the world that you were 'someone' or to prove that your way was right. You were powerful and manipulative, and at times enjoyed being deliberately obtuse and obstinate because you loved to control. However, you now know better – it's pride in doing a good job or working through some difficult issue that turns you on. You are happy to be a fly on the wall. You're free to get on with your inner soul work without the intrusion of daily life.

Your task is to remind yourself that you are a part of everyone and everyone is a part of you. This may be difficult with your powerful sense of self-possession because you can clash with the wills of others. However, you are able to connect with the greater concept of soul while being as practical as a bumblebee. You can see the great and small in life and you recognize that everything is a mirror, 'as above so below'.

Your soul guides you to re-assess and check your life carefully, and regularly, on every level – physically, emotionally and mentally – and to re-evaluate for spiritual growth. Sometimes you get stuck in a deep soul pattern that's hard to let go of. You're so stubborn and rigid that you can sabotage success and forward movement. However, constant re-evaluation enables you to melt away your resistance so that you accept life the way it is.

Soul Vibration 9

Your soul yearns for cosmic equality – to be able to recognize that all the different levels of consciousness, behaviour, soul qualities and karmic lessons within humanity and the universe are actually within yourself. You see past the horizon; you can see the beginning of a situation and the end (its potential). You're very psychic. You are able to access higher states of awareness within, and go into altered states of consciousness for periods of time that leave you smiling and wondering.

You're incredibly practical, capable and sensible. You accept everything that comes your way in life – nothing fazes you. You make room in your heart and soul for every person on the planet, without prejudice. Compassion is your first and last name. You possess such a broad outlook on life and you really know how to apply it, through hard work, devotion, service and plain giving.

People may not notice your soul shining because, like a hermit, you will hide away from attention. You camouflage yourself in groups, at parties or at home, by putting the emphasis on what you're doing rather than have people pointing at you. As a result, you may drop out of college or even withdraw from society, as part of your growth, until you realize that demonstrating practical wisdom in everyday life is your mission. Every day, in every part of the world, more compassion and love is needed to give to others, and you do your best.

In the past (or past lives) you were like a pirate living off your nerves and you didn't know how to piece together your own life let alone be able to help anyone else. You may have been ignorant about the workings of your soul. Perhaps you became over-indulgent materially, sexually or in other ways. Now you are quite happy to shed your skin regularly, to adapt to your own and others' soul values, and to include everyone in your vision of equality. The dark times taught you resilience and self-reliance, and you are free to wander where you choose. Now you are very measured and discriminating about what needs to be done.

CHAPTER 6

What gifts and lessons can I discover from my names?

(Name Numbers & Karmic Key Numbers)

Names are wonderful – they help you to explore your individual identity and also connect you to the divine because all names are sounds from soul. Some names resonate with you and lift you up, while others that you may encounter can turn you stone cold. For example, you may love a friend's unusual name, but your sister cringes when she hears it! The reason you are attracted to, or repulsed by, certain names is purely your own particular make-up and your soul experiences from the past (or past lives). You may also love some names because you see numerological qualities in them that you like or want to see in yourself, or vice versa. For example, you may be over-caring at times, and therefore people with Name Number 6 may irritate you because they can be like that too. Names are energies, but people serve as mirrors so you can recognize all the different aspects of yourself, and find more wholeness and harmony in life.

When you add up the letter values from your complete birth names you arrive at your Name Number, which can bring insights into gifts, vocation, career, physical attributes, health patterns, karmic lessons (responsibilities) and relationships. But there is far more to discover. The numbers missing from your full birth names, your Karmic Key Numbers, help you to identify qualities you've used in the past, or past lives, that can help to improve your life now.

How can I use names in Numerology?

So why do we need names in the first place? Names help us to objectify life so that we can see parts of ourselves in the mirror, so we know what that particular type of energy is about and then we can use it for good. Names give us opportunities to look at so many different aspects of ourselves and provide us with an abundance of lessons, gifts and qualities to enrich everyday life. For example, you may have a range of gifts, with words and communication, with laughter and joy, with hard work and personal responsibility, and so on. Recognizing the many different facets of the names on your birth certificate, nicknames, married name, the name you choose to go by after divorce, stage names and any others can offer you a multi-dimensional choice of vibrations to help you live an inspiring and fulfilling life.

When names are sounded many times they build up energy that becomes even more potent in terms of their influence. For example, the name James is one of the most timeless and popular names in the Western world. Translating each of the letters in the name James from the alphabet (1 1 4 5 1) you can see that they add up to 12 → 1 + 2 = 3 (sacrifice, giving, joy, inspiration, creativity, the blueprint). Given that this name is said so often, its Number 3 energy and qualities are all the more significant for humanity as a soul group as well as for personal growth.

Although people with the same name or Name Number will have similar qualities, they will apply the energies in completely different ways depending on other influences from the Birth Chart such as the Personality and Life Purpose Numbers, which will naturally be different. The Name Numbers and date of birth all interact together too. Even the place of someone's birth can affect the experiences they may have.

TRYIT WORKING OUT YOUR NAME NUMBERS

Name Numbers are calculated by adding up the letter values in the name. (These values are listed on page 27.)

There are many Name Numbers. Your first name generates your Goal Number, which highlights your personal goals and behaviour and sometimes reveals deeper aspirational qualities. Your middle names are Support Names providing you with a reserve of qualities to call upon during times of need. Your surname or Family Name Number brings important lessons that your whole family line have been working on together. The full birth names highlight karmic (or past life) responsibilities, physical traits, vocational qualities and gifts.

The full names on your birth certificate provide you with an exact karmic toolbox of lessons and gifts that you've acquired In the past (or past lives). Their influence is profound upon your physical attributes, relationships and vocation. The full birth names are given to you synchronistically for the greater good of your whole genetic and soul group. Hence, the process of naming a baby is a responsibility that, for some people, weighs heavily upon the family and particularly the

Example. Luke Adam Peterson:

Luke 3 + 3 + 2 + 5 = 13 → 1 + 3 = 4
Luke's Goal Number is 4.

Adam 1 + 4 + 1 + 4 = 10 → 1 + 0 = 1
His Support Name Number is 1.

Peterson 7 + 5 + 2 + 5 + 9 + 1 + 6 + 5 = 40 → 4 + 0 = 4
The Peterson Family Name Number is 4.

Luke's complete Name Number is 4 + 1 + 4 = 9.

parents. But don't worry – the appropriate names for the soul of the newborn, and for the advancement of the group, always materialize perfectly.

Many people change their names later in life, often out of personal desire to better themselves. It can also be because there are hidden underlying fears of the qualities in the full birth names. Or there is a resistance to taking ownership of the journey, perhaps because something 'negative' has happened and there is a desire to run away, or they may be trying to disown a part of themselves that actually needs healing, in which case it could help to turn inward and really connect with their name vibrations and soul. Numerology can help you to pinpoint what issues of this sort are all about and help you turn your life around. (You can read more detailed information about name-changing in my book *Choose The Perfect Baby Name*.)

What happens if a name is in another language?

In this book we use the roman alphabet, but if you cannot write a name from another language in these letters then go by the sound it makes. Sound is vibration or soul. For example, if a letter sounds like 'f', treat it as a number 6. It's important to listen to how your name is pronounced and which part of the word is emphasized. Everything is information that shows us how we are connected to others, to soul and to life.

What qualities are associated with particular Name Numbers?

Name Number 1

You're ambitious for your creativity to be used up each day. Your creative mind is so expansive that it can conjure up millions of new ideas and inventions daily, which you're only too willing to pass on to others.

You can be very bullish and rip apart stagnant situations in a harmless way to create positive change. You may blurt out the obvious (which sometimes leaves people reeling) or you may even consciously flatten them verbally so they have to pick themselves up off the floor. However, often you have such an innocence about you that you don't even notice the results of your words or actions. You have a powerful temper but, as always, your daily environment will mirror back to you important issues that you need to address within yourself.

You tend to run off an empty tank health-wise, and you may experience great adrenalin highs and lows, which also play havoc with your energy levels.

Psychologically, you tend to hold on to emotions and contain yourself to the point of explosion. This repression can contribute to extreme frustration or even violent outbursts at times. Exercise can be useful in this respect as you need to learn to channel your energy positively and creatively.

Your family are working through issues of intimacy (on many levels) and hence you may live at a great distance away from each other. Perhaps you avoid family gatherings where you may be required to talk about personal issues. Paradoxically you may be (psychologically) attached to your parents' apron strings even if you're a parent yourself.

Name Number 2

You're very ambitious for peace. Your gift is your mediation skill – you're brilliant at calming down situations; when your friends are arguing and being over-emotional you know just what to say. However, you don't like being put on the spot and having to choose sides, which is why you don't always savour being in the position of the go-between.

You're a real softie with a heart of gold and a kind word to say about everyone – a warm soul. But the nectar is hidden within and sometimes you put a tough exterior on display to the world to protect yourself. You may be afraid of rejection. However, you are able to remain gloriously open to relationships and to life. You've learned to listen, which helps you through situations, and you do communicate in a simple way what's going on.

Your family may be sensitive souls who can read each other's feelings and offer comfort and security by reaching out to one another. You may relish the feeling that you are the wise owl in the family and reject others' wisdom in a defensive way. However, you enjoy debating and deliberating – it's your family's way of working things out and reaching equilibrium.

Name Number 3

You're ambitious about finding inspiration in life. You're always seeking out situations that can uplift you and in which you can use your inner being to uplift others (one of your gifts.) You simply love life, the ups and even all the downs, because you know there is always something more to learn. You possess a 'backpacker' attitude – you take each day exactly as it comes and then make the most of it.

Your family may be exhibitionists or natural entertainers. While another family member making light of a problem can be a real gift to uplift the soul, there is a time and place for everything. As a family you know you are always ready for action, and ready to demonstrate the love that you share.

You are brimming with self-confidence and are by nature an optimist. But psychologically you can sometimes be incredibly cynical, criticize the world for all its faults and moan over things you don't like about yourself. This can be hard work until, through inner reflection, the sunshine breaks through the clouds. You know yourself well, and on days when you've lost your sense of humour, you can seek the answers within. Indeed, you cannot remain down for long because you've got far too much to enjoy and experience in life.

Name Number 4

You're ambitious to build an empire. This empire is not necessarily for you but for the whole world – you may be involved in demanding charity work, for example. Developing your vision sometimes takes time, but you possess soul endurance and mental determination and you simply carry on until the end result has been achieved. Sometimes when you bring all the 'tools' together you realize that you need to be more realistic with your approach. Though it is the striving for something and the journey that's important, it's even better when tangible results can be seen at the end of the day.

You've learned to be reliable when others ask you for help, but you can sometimes doubt whether to help someone in the first place. You are down to earth and resilient, and are always seeking practical solutions to problems, but not everybody is the same. You make friends for life and your loyalty will encourage you to help people if you can. You are practical with your healthcare regime, and take care to look after yourself to ensure that you can give of your best.

Family life is sacred to you and it usually forms the foundation of your very existence. You may meet regularly – at the same place every day, week or month – and do the same things that you love doing together. Routine provides you all with security and continuity. However, there can be dramatic upsets. Change is the enemy because it makes you fear the future. Your family goal is responsibility, so you know that essentially you can all prosper and grow on your own.

Name Number 5

You're ambitious to explore the unknown. This can take on many shapes and forms – studying psychology and the workings of the mind or going on an adventure holiday around the world. Relationships are a big part of the unknown waiting for you, and you go there. You possess emotional intelligence that enables you to get close to others at a deeper level. Making connections is your gift. You're incredibly observant and can always find the tiniest bit of information to brighten up your day.

Your witty observations on life and your quick, dry sense of humour are invigorating and stimulate people to think or to do a double-take sometimes – did they really just hear that? While you enjoy being shocking you are prepared to tone down the atmosphere and spare others' blushes by shutting up at times.

Your family may be very meticulous about details but sometimes they make too much fuss over nothing. It's great to be like that in a day job where precision really counts, but it can be tedious otherwise. Your family may also fluctuate in and out of each other's lives, because you're all so deeply involved with your own lives!

You know what it means to live life on the edge, and it has helped you to grow into a deeper, more sensitive human being. You are committed to your soul's journey. Psychologically, you can be irrational, irresponsible and erratic at times. Curiosity about life gets the better of you, but soul always leads you back home.

Name Number 6

You're ambitious for quality time. Quality time for you as a soul is always going to be your biggest priority. By internalizing and connecting within you can gain a bigger perspective on life. Quality time with friends and family is a major concern too. You're a team player and like to feel you have an important role to play within the group. Finally, you seek quality time to do the work you need to do.

You may be completely devoted to a relationship, career, diet, or to a specific religion, and you're service orientated – you give yourself fully. For you there's no second best and you can become quite exclusive with your attitude and actions. Psychologically you may lash out at others emotionally when situations don't go as perfectly as you dreamed. This is due to the depth of your emotions and because of your attachment to an outcome. You can be romantic, sentimental and cry at the slightest thing, but you keep on giving and loving – that is your goal.

Your family may be service-orientated, traditional and conservative. They may place great emphasis on being seen to be a strong family unit, even if they're not. Your family may be welcoming or excluding according to their moods, and you never know until the moment. Your family like to keep in touch by email, by sending letters in the post, or by telephoning, but they may infinitely prefer to exchange photographs as they are very visual, aesthetic and creative.

Health-wise, you are up on the latest trends in nutrition, exercise and beauty regimes, and although you may give up once the next wave comes along at least you try. You like to preserve your energy for what's important each day, and will work hard at keeping the harmony between body and soul.

Name Number 7

You're ambitious to materialize change. Even on days when nothing seems to be happening on the surface there is a lot going on underneath. Your gift is to bring soul to life, and you have learned to be used for the greater good. Perhaps you write music that inspires the creativity of others, or spend time listening to Puccini, Mozart or some stunning operatic aria.

Health-wise, you can crumble emotionally, as you are vulnerable and delicate at times. You have a vivid imagination and you regularly convince yourself a headache is something worse than it is. When you are under the weather, you also trust your instincts and often turn to herbs, good nutrition and a good night's sleep to restore your energy. You may be an advocate for using conventional and alternative doctors and treatments, which you feel work really well hand in hand.

Your family may be busy people leading their own lives, so you may just wave to each other on your smart phones from different locations around the globe from time to time. Occasionally you may actually forget you have any family at all because you're all so absorbed in your own lives anyway.

Name Number 8
You're ambitious for guidance. You may attend a course on 'how to be successful in business' or a seminar on 'positive thinking', but ultimately you know the best guidance comes from within. Spirituality permeates every moment and every

aspect of daily life, but you can actively access the power
and strength of this unseen energy by connecting with soul.
Intuition speaks to you at all times of the day and night.
You are receptive and connect with the flow of the
universal energies passing through you.

You may take power seriously and use psychological
seduction techniques to control others. You may be very
selective about who you spend your time with. You want
to be the best and to bolster your chances of winning in
life. However, your soul is happiest when it's full of love,
and eventually you invest more time into empowering and
fostering successful honest relationships, which is your gift.

Your family may be shrewd 'salt of the earth' people who
have really lived. You can enjoy the benefits of material
pleasures, but you've balanced this out with love, because
you all know what really matters. Ultimately, you know that
spirit is in charge and that you are all being steered along
the wheel of fate, learning important lessons about
responsibility like everybody else.

Name Number 9

You're ambitious for equality. You may even be a
campaigner who is passionate about everything on the
planet – the plants, the insects, the animals and the people.

Perhaps you live your life by setting a good example and treating others with great dignity and respect, and being as fair, honest and inclusive as you can. You are compassionate and even when people hurt you in some way, you can still take a step back and see life from their point of view. If your neighbour has had an affair with your partner, you may take the view that that's what their souls needed. You may believe in past lives and the journey of the soul, and possess a big vision for humanity. Your life is about service and giving.

Your family possess a fair sense of what's right and wrong and there has to be a star in your family who becomes something like a barrister, humanitarian or a powerful campaigner. It's important for your family group to shine.

Health-wise, you may experience aches and pains from exhaustion and putting too much pressure on yourself. Being discriminating about what you can take on may mean you need to let some aspects of life go. Quiet time is so valuable for you to decide about what's important.

Psychologically you can be awkward and difficult to please because you have such high expectations of life – you may be particularly difficult to live or work with. You are an idealist who sees the best potential in people, yet they don't always deliver. However, you may experience many disappointments until you let go of expectation and accept life as it is.

Which other name-related numbers can I investigate?

Your Karmic Key Numbers are discovered by working out what numbers are missing from your full birth names or from the full names by which you were very first known (see page 105 for further explanation).

In many countries birth names are supplemented by additional religious or spiritual names, extra family names, generic cultural names and so on. You can explore the wonderful qualities and meanings of all your names, but to arrive at the Karmic Key Number you need to know what your original birth names were. These provide the karmic influences from the whole journey of your soul from previous lifetimes. The names you attract at birth therefore provide you with a mirror to the past.

Understanding karma means taking responsibility for yourself and your journey through life. It's about recognizing why something has happened so that you can turn the issue around. Sometimes this takes time, but more often than not a short, sharp realization shifts your perspective and changes life forever. Karma is ultimately positive because it brings you more into harmony (and alignment) within yourself, the world and even with the greater universe.

Your Karmic Key Numbers provide major lessons and qualities you've worked on before (in the past or in past lives). By recognizing and embracing the qualities of your missing numbers you can free up energy so you can become more attractive and creative in life.

What can I learn from my Karmic Key Numbers?

So why look at your Karmic Key Numbers? You may go through life feeling as though you're just not getting some important message, or you keep repeating deep patterns and you don't know why when the answer is staring you in the face. You may also feel there's always something missing from life and so spend your time running around looking for it on the outside when all the answers are there already.

Many people do not like to look at the past; they feel it is just that, the past, or they do not like to look at themselves perhaps because it's too painful. But the passport to your future success is built on the past that has made you into who you are today. Indeed, you may be content and happy with your life now. But by embracing key qualities of yourself from the past, you can recognize, learn, let go, and become even more at home and inspired by life.

What qualities are associated with particular Karmic Key Numbers?

Karmic Key Number 1

You are willing to be reborn, and to give birth to your inner soul wisdom. Your light is strong and powerful, and you are able to illuminate the darkest recesses of your mind to find the truth. You are a visionary. People see you as a leader or some kind of spiritual warrior clearing the way for others to find the path and to follow. Original and inventive, you come up with new ideas that are ahead of their time. You've learned to relate ideas to reality.

You are forceful and strong, and find it hard to give way to right and reason. You need to check your morals and intentions regularly. You can be out of touch with reality because you focus a lot of energy on yourself. You can sometimes be petty over issues that have no major consequence, bullish about getting what you want and occasionally walk over others to achieve goals.

Karmic Key Number 2

You are willing to allow the burning heat of spirit to purify your mind and emotions so that your soul can grow. You welcome spiritual transformation. You use your wisdom to help others. You channel your intense creativity into worthwhile projects. You are a good listener, and are receptive to new ideas and change. You co-operate with others and engage in collaborative exchanges to benefit the world. You find compromise easy – you can see the other's point of view. You are a peacemaker and mediator, and are able to make good decisions quickly. You think of others, and are easy to be around because you're completely open to life. You've learned to put yourself in other people's shoes.

You can sometimes be manipulative and demanding, and deliberately inflict emotional pain on others. You also wallow in separation at times; being cocooned in your own space is safer than reaching out as you feel easily rejected. Others you meet may be sent off balance because you can be highly strung. You deny your feelings or fall into apathy and inertia, and are unable to make decisions. You find it difficult to nurture yourself or others. You can be defensive.

Karmic Key Number 3

You are willing to dive into your soul and go with the flow along the river of life. You take everyone along with you for the ride, your love and joy of life spreading out to those around you. You are free with your love, have a generosity of soul and see the sunshine even on cloudy days. You've learned to be more generous in life.

You can have a twisted outlook on life at times, which can cause you to jump into situations without thinking them through well enough. To do so you need to learn to focus on facts and reflect within and also to recognize that you sometimes amble through life with no particular aim, taking a rather superficial view of things. You may be quick to criticize yourself or judge others. In these respects you can be very gushing or reckless.

Karmic Key Number 4

You are willing to break open your fundamental outlook or routine to make room for new soul growth. You are conscientious and good at organizing and can make others feel special. You never give up on your friends – you're a rock and are able to offer constructive criticism. You take care of the basic responsibilities, which takes care of life. You're an inspired 'artist' and are passionate about what you do, which brings you a strong work ethic. You've learned to be patient and practical.

But at times hesitancy can lose you the deal as you search for reassurance to ease your insecurities. You create dramas over nothing. You cling on to old possessions and money for dear life. You can thus be resistant to change, but you take risks that you know will cause problems from the outset. When you do, the whole area of personal responsibility doesn't exist.

Karmic Key Number 5

You are willing to become more conscious as a soul and explore life fully. Your clarity of speech is breathtaking – people get the truth instantly, in part because you take a systematic approach to situations and can find a needle in a haystack. You keep an open mind even when people are trying to cloud your vision. Another beneficial quality is that you are very telepathic and sense when others are going to phone, or come into or out of your life. You're always on the move – your energy speeds up other's vibrations. You've learned to apply common sense.

At times you're quick to jump to conclusions with your restless mind getting lost in the details. You can be unpredictable in love, money and other respects. This flightiness means you're impossible to pin down to commitments. You are sceptical and dismissive of others' achievements, while for yourself you talk a load of hot air to impress others with what you 'know'.

Karmic Key Number 6

You are willing to give over your personal desires to focus on what's important: soul growth. To this end you are generous and kind-hearted, welcoming and warm. You love being in love, but giving love is your priority and your encouragement helps others to blossom. You like to look your best, yet recognize that true beauty shines from within. You're generous and kind. You've learned to follow the golden rules – compassion, respect and service.

You may abuse yourself and others. You may try to turn all situations to your advantage. You are very spoiled and a real heart-breaker. At times you neglect people's feelings or needs, but paradoxically you may smother others with the appearance of love because you just want your needs met.

Karmic Key Number 7

You are willing to use your earthly and soul gifts to benefit others. You're a catalyst for change; you move people and situations on without even realizing. Multi-talented and able to use many of your gifts all at once, you're also a deep thinker who can deliver the goods. You love peace and solitude, especially being out and about in nature, and this can help you find your own truth. Your intuition serves others well and you're generally spot on. You've learned not to take things personally.

You want to fit in but you can cause controversy and be paranoid because you may delude yourself about reality and dream your life away. You need to learn to steady your nerves, and to have patience. This will help you not to be so easily misunderstood. You're too fussy about cleanliness and being clean (in all its connotations).

Karmic Key Number 8

You are willing to be guided, and guide others to the best of your abilities. You are like a thunderbolt waking people up to see life as it is, but in the process you demonstrate humility, great charisma and charm. You are talented at organization and business, enjoying delegating responsibilities. You look to yourself for inner strength rather than relying on others. You've learned to be humble.

You desire fame and recognition and are prone to keeping everything for yourself and being greedy. You need to learn to give up ownership and taking yourself too seriously. Irresponsibility and bullying others into giving you what you want are also issues.

Karmic Key Number 9

You are willing to allow the power of spiritual transformation to work through you and you go along with the process. You let go of the past and have few needs because of your unshakeable faith in goodness. You accept people for who they are and you're very understanding, though you like everything out in the open. You've learned to find your identity.

You are naive and attached to receiving praise, but despite that you feel superior and are bitter about giving up your time for others. You need to learn to talk without preaching. You're narrow-minded attitude excludes others and restricts your experience of life. You may be arrogant and pompous and get a kick out of humiliating others. Your high expectations may cause disappointments.

CHAPTER 7

How do numbers related to dates influence my everyday life?

(General Dates & Personal Year Numbers)

The numbers in the date have a far-reaching effect on us and life. The General (or Collective) Date Number is calculated from any date (see box opposite for information) and influences everyone in the world that day, colouring all our experiences.

Each individual's Personal Year Number (derived from the date of their last birthday) influences relationships, health, lifestyle, career, spiritual growth, creative potential, and the timing of events. Although as always, it's up to us how we choose to apply these energies.

What characteristics are associated with General Date Numbers?

Qualities associated with particular numbers in the 1 to 9 sequence are explained in *Focus On: Interpreting the numbers 1 to 9* in Chapter 1, page 24. All Dates are formed out of the same cycles or numbers 1 to 9. Each number provides a key characteristic or focus:

1 Opportunities   6 Completion
2 Decisions   7 Fusion
3 Plans   8 Re-evaluation
4 Structure   9 Transformation
5 Changes

What use are Personal Year Numbers?

The function of the Personal Year Cycles 1 to 9 is for you to learn from both the past and the present. You can also tap into the hidden creative potential contained within each number to create a brighter future for yourself and the world.

The Personal Year Cycles can also help raise consciousness and bring humanity together. As you delve within yourself to connect with your soul through your Personal Year Number, it increases awareness, and when a lot of people do that it can have a really positive ripple effect within society. Individuality is important – your qualities, skills, gifts and talents are there to be used, but they are designed for sharing with the group.

Each Cycle flows into the next. So when you are in a 6 Year you are being influenced by a little of the Numbers 5 and 7 too. You may notice this when you have a birthday. You may particularly feel a little heavy just before some birthdays. Perhaps you become melancholic, sentimental or frustrated because you are now hurrying to complete some of the issues you were working on during the last 'Personal Year'. This is a great time to embark on soul searching and letting go. Sometimes you can feel the influence of your new Personal Year vibration maybe even three or four

TRYIT **WORKING OUT YOUR PERSONAL YEAR NUMBER**

Your Personal Year Number is calculated using the date of your last birthday.

Example. If Anne's most recent birthday was on 26.12.2016:

26 + 12 + 2 + 0 + 1 + 6 = 47 → 11 = 1 + 1 = 2.

This means that, from 26 December 2016 to 25 December 2017, Anne's Personal Year Number is 2.

weeks before your birthday; if you've already cleared the experiences from the old year you're ready for the new.

When you know what Personal Year Number is influencing you, you realize that what is actually happening is how it's really meant to be. For example, you may start throwing things away from your wardrobe suddenly and then discover you're in Personal Year 9, which relates to letting go and moving on.

Life improves if you are willing to learn, to grow and to embrace change. The Personal Year Cycles 1 to 9 can guide you through every stage of your life so that you can make the most out of your journey. They are positive signposts to the past, present and future.

What qualities are associated with particular Personal Year Numbers?

Personal Year Number 1

You're entering a new domain. Everything may seem strange for a while, even though life is stimulating. You can find it difficult to relate to family, friends or colleagues as you normally do because something in you has changed. You may start thinking in a different way or behave out of character. This may be quite perplexing for all concerned.

You probably think it's the world and its people that have shifted, not you, and avidly look outside yourself for answers.

In a 1 Cycle you're being asked to take a fresh approach to life, to bring new energy and ideas out into the light of day. You're developing a new perspective on life. There may be an external event that inspires you to change your view, like a change in your health status or the death of someone close to you. But this is simply a mirror for the process going on inside of you. You experience a sense of rebirth – with new opportunities, vitality, and a renewed interest in life.

If you hide yourself away during a 1 Cycle it may be because you're still processing issues from the previous nine years and going through inner transformation. Loved ones may have a job pulling you out of your self-imposed isolation or withdrawn state. You may avoid intimate relationships during this phase. Eventually life moves you on as the new 1 energy takes hold.

During this time, you're looking for inner guidance to find out what your soul purpose is. Issues of personal power can crop up during a 1 Cycle as you look to assert yourself in all ways. For example, you may act bullishly, focus on money, or wear yourself out pounding your body at an exercise class. This is because you are setting your intentions for relationships, lifestyle and career for the next nine years.

Personal Year Number 2

If you've asserted yourself in Personal Year 1 and connected with your inner drive, now you're ready to open up to life. Openness is all about being receptive to life and being prepared to listen instead of shutting off your ears and hiding. Life Is kind if you can see the kindness.

So you're going to feel your way through situations and experiences this year, and you are going to be much more sensitive to the energy around. It may feel as though your strings are being pulled in two different directions at once and you're in the middle. It can be a rocky time with your emotions flying high and your moods fluctuating rapidly. But you're looking for balance and you're also in touch with your inner wisdom, so you're aware of the fluctuations.

Personal Year 2 is a great time for bonding in relationships, with your child, a lover, a friend, but more importantly with your own soul. You feel more love than you've ever felt possible, and you're opening your heart and blossoming like a lotus flower as you look for your soul-mate.

You can be needy at times or feel as though you're starving for emotional closeness. Conversely, you might shut off emotionally or reject others who try to get close to you. In fact it's a great time to face your fears and throw caution to the wind if you've been holding yourself back from making important decisions.

Sexually, you want cuddles and deep communication more than anything, but with your heart so open, making love feels like pure ecstasy – two become one. You're seeking a partner you can grow with both spiritually and emotionally. In this 2 Personal Year your aim is to keep life simple.

Personal Year Number 3
You've found your direction and purpose in Year 1. You weighed up wisely and made important decisions about your life in Year 2. Now you're entering a Personal Year 3, which can bring great expansion if good plans are set in place. Life is moving you on, and you make the most of each day living, loving and growing, or you can create more chaos by being scatty and unfocused. Get a grip.

You may feel as though you're back in the playground because your inner child rises to the surface. If you're normally a serious person or have been burdened down with too many responsibilities this is very refreshing. Perhaps you haven't laughed for ages, but now you find pure joy at the end of the tunnel. You may feel the urge to express yourself in many different ways during Personal Year 3, perhaps by playing the piano or another musical instrument, taking up writing a diary, attending a cookery or massage class, expressing your opinions and feelings more often, becoming more affectionate with loved ones, and so on.

From a deeper perspective it's time to learn to be your true self, and learn to be in the moment. If life falls apart for a while it's because you're letting go of old aspects of you that are no longer needed, so that the plan for your future can be revealed.

Sexually, you are at your most confident and may be willing to dress up and indulge in fun and frolics, but remember that it's time for some hard self-reflection to make sure you're clued up about what you're really doing within all areas of your life.

Personal Year Number 4

You've set your plans alight in Personal Year 3, now it's time to anchor them firmly in the earth and to lay foundations. For example, you may have already met the person of your dreams, bonded and fallen deeply in love. In Year 3 you became restless and reflected upon the real purpose of relationships. Now in Personal Year 4 the question is: are you going to cement new relationships by taking them to the next level? Maybe you will buy a property together, get married, and so on, or simply deepen your love and soul connection.

Life is never boring but it can get monotonous if you don't want to change and if you seek familiarity in a security blanket. If you're stuck in a rut it can feel almost impossible to pull yourself out of it. But during this cycle all you need to do is to take one step at a time. Life will create the changes that are needed as long as you are making an effort. Money and material matters concern you most, but try to broaden your awareness – get innovative with your thoughts and ideas.

This is also a time for radical spiritual growth and inner changes, but it's up to you to go for it. In this 4 Year you may find a relationship or business suddenly anchors and grows, or plans you've made simply fade away because your vision and actions in the last 3 Year weren't fit for purpose. Life may be asking you to get back to basics and strip everything back (physically, emotionally, intellectually) to see what's truly needed. Reflecting inward toward your soul can help you connect with the spiritual impulse to carry on, especially during heavy weather.

Sex can be passionate and fiery when you feel safe with your partner. You may go back to your roots to find a lover from the past – loyalty and friendship last forever. While there can be conflicts of responsibility in relationships, you're actually growing up and laying down a solid platform to launch your future from, so you are being thorough.

Personal Year Number 5

Life is movement and change, and Personal Year Number 5 reminds you that, like the weather, nothing stays the same forever. This is quite reassuring, especially if in your Year 4 you got 'stuck' in patterns and entrenched in situations or issues. Life will now move you on spectacularly, whether in short sharp shocks or via a gale-force wind.

How your mind perceives information can alter radically this year, too, in order to free up space for the future. This can be painful and tricky as it may require you to connect to some elements of the past that you'd rather forget. But, as the saying goes: you can run but you can't hide. You may therefore be forced to look within. Deep emotional cleansing can leave you feeling sparkling clean, shiny and magnetic.

You may receive exciting news that requires you to make urgent changes to your relationships, career or lifestyle. It's a time to spring back to life; perhaps you feel as though you've just woken up out of a deep sleep and suddenly life is speeding and whirling again.

Sexually, you want a lover who keeps you guessing, and you aim to create a veil of mystery about yourself too. You want sexual self-gratification, but bringing soul and love into the equation enhances your satisfaction further. Sweet talk will get you everywhere! This year is also great for personal networking generally, connecting with life at a deeper soul level, and for powerful change. You need to keep communicating and exchanging ideas in order to keep things fresh in all areas of your life.

Personal Year Number 6

Everything is hitting a peak and with so much going on it feels as though a huge mix of emotions is swirling around inside of you and you're in a state of pure flux. You may feel as though life is turning you upside down and inside out. Life may smell of roses, yet at some point you're going to need to start fishing around beneath the surface. You're looking for the real meaning of life – love. Perhaps you fall hopelessly in love with love, or have your heart broken. Either way you're learning to feel and to contact your inner self or soul during this 6 Year.

This year timing is crucial. Perhaps you suddenly notice your biological clock ticking away, and are there really enough hours in the day? So you're on a steep learning curve about time management. You can't go to dance class, work on a project, and look after the kids all at the same time. But if you take a step back and look at the whole picture you realize you can at least fit all those items into your day. You're learning to become a good manager, which requires you to put the team first, and to include yourself in the group.

You're also learning to honour your promises and you know the choices you make influence others. Likewise, when you take on commitments, you need to know what you're letting yourself in for. Look at your choices in life. Do you go for first-class living, expensive perfumes and spending days at the beauty parlour with life solely revolving around yourself, or do you learn to give of your inner beauty, love and wisdom to the world? As long as you're happy with your choice that's what's important.

Sexually, you spend quality time with your lover. Love-making sessions engage all your senses and you refuse to be rushed. You may be in denial about your own needs or refuse to accept others' needs too – but look to your soul for answers. Relationships are under the spotlight. You keep wanting more and more, but instead of taking advantage of situations, fill your heart with love, and your cup will be full to the top.

Personal Year Number 7

There is a dichotomy during this 7 Cycle. A part of you dives into happy isolation and craves solitude. Here you have the liberty to internalize, to explore your mind, emotions and your soul through meditation, walks in the park and quiet reflection. You want your space from others at this time because you're more prone to taking on their emotions and you may find them difficult to process simultaneously with your own inner explorations. The other part of you, however, is out in the world, making deals, singing songs, matchmaking friends, working on the cutting edge of business, being progressive and making things happen.

You can go from one extreme to another and you need to learn to be aware of the moment because your thoughts and actions can become destructive. For example, if you embark upon too much isolation you may get lost from reality, and if you focus on the outer world too much you may get lost in the illusion that the physical world is all there is. You're learning to blend your soul and your personality together so that you can find the middle ground.

You're likely to feel emotionally fragile and empty at times, but this makes you more available to see the truth. Indeed, you can even seem blunt, aloof or emotionally cold, but people will know it's just a phase you're going through. You may become more fearful of pain (of all types) or of going into relationships or life deeply because you feel it's going to bring you even more pain. This paradoxically makes for a creative period because you can channel your feelings into writing, cooking or expressing yourself clearly to loved ones.

Sexually, you want to fuse mind, body and soul with your lover. You're looking for total ecstasy – the connection of spirit with nature is mind-blowing. You're a trailblazer in relationships, instigating change, exploring your identity and you can be full of your own self-importance (but you know it). Check your psychic instincts; sensitivity and intuition can show you what's real and important in life.

Personal Year Number 8

You're ready to stand up on your own and look the world directly in the eye. You don't need anyone else to fight your battles because you've surrendered to your soul. You still want to be successful with all your projects, but you also want everyone else to win. You're dropping your ego's need for competition and instead you're happy to put all your energy into simply being yourself, using your gifts and going for life.

You're intent on reorganizing everything in your environment, which can be testing for others. And you can be over-assertive, controlling and want things too much on your terms at times, which can be challenging. Rigidity and pig-headedness can sabotage your goals quite spectacularly so it's important to re-evaluate regularly. Revisiting the past can show you how far you've moved on, but there's always more work to do.

Sexually, you like to play games in the bedroom. You're either full on hot and amorous or cool and passive – you enjoy both roles. You're revisiting all kinds of incredible memories from the past, some happy, some painful, and identifying what the deeper message is along the way. You remember Personal Year 1 – where you began this journey, and you're doing your best to align your vision and see how it sums up in reality (maybe more re-evaluating to do).

Personal Year Number 9

This year it's like you've got ants in your pants and you can't sit still. You may get an urgent itch to throw things away and to 'clear out cupboards' on many different levels. It's an ideal time to lighten your load and move on, whether through choice or pure circumstance. If, for example, your boss has called time on your job or your lover has disappeared into the dusty distance, then you need to bring in the quality of pure acceptance. You are, however, capable of exploring issues that have arisen during the last nine years – you can learn from life. Your soul is gaining so much wisdom as you grow and it's going to stand you in good stead in your next nine-year cycle just ahead.

Hidden secrets may be gloriously or awkwardly revealed this year – perhaps you need to come clean and get something off your chest or things may happen without your consent. These situations are powerful, and can be overpowering for all concerned, but there are no real mistakes as such because everyone and everything is intrinsically connected through divine synchronicity. Indeed, as you withdraw into your soul, you can process all the feelings of shame, guilt, fear and pain from the past and recognize how they've helped you to grow. You're also learning to accept yourself and others, and are giving yourself permission to do what you must, knowing that life is all a learning experience.

Life comes full circle, but with each turn of the cycle you grow and see and experience life in a different way. You may have a penchant for research and gaining practical knowledge during this year. Or you may call upon your compassion and understanding to help you serve humanity in some way. From this you may develop a passion for the environment, humanitarian issues, the community, equality, sport or education, and immerse yourself by forming or joining forces with groups.

Sexually, anything goes – your only aim is to please your lover. You're broadening your horizons in the bedroom as well as in life in general, so things are looking up. Your worldliness has expanded – your soul is now richer from experience at the end of this nine-year journey. There's no turning back, nowhere to go because you're already home (in your soul). You're living life in the moment.

CHAPTER 8

Can Numerology help me
make a wider contribution
to society?

(Master Numbers)

Master Numbers (see below for how to identify these) in Numerology are among the best guides to help not only individuals but also the whole of humanity to grow. Identifying and aligning with these numbers helps us – as a group – to rise to higher levels of awareness and together to reach for oneness with the divine. At any one time, there are millions of people around the planet waking up to their collective responsibilities and consciousness, and group energy has a far stronger influence than any individual. Even if we feel different or separate, or think the opposite, the love and soul connection between us all is always there.

What are Master Numbers?

A Master Number is a number that is doubled: 11, 22, 33, and so on up to 99. You may notice them in your age, or in significant words, names or dates, or in calculating some of the Numbers covered in preceding chapters. They can pop up everywhere in life. When a single digit appears twice in a row like this the related energies become much more intense and a choice arises to align with the energies in a different way: to serve humanity as they represent the highest possible attainment of the vibration. Placed next to each other like this, the repeated numbers represent 'as above so below' hence they're often also referred to as 'Mirror Numbers', with one number representing personality (or the outer world) and the other representing the soul (or inner world).

The Master Numbers 11, 22 and 33 are the most significant because they represent the Trinity (Soul, Spirit, Nature are one). Number 3 always provides the blueprint in life. If you have these numbers in your reading you are being called to service and will automatically be required to put others first. Master Numbers can sometimes be difficult to process because they rock the boat, but they always provide great opportunities for personal and collective growth and success. Even if you only channel 0.1 per cent of their energy, you are contributing to soul growth or the brotherhood of man.

As mentioned a moment ago, we can find the Master Numbers 11 to 99 in all kinds of areas in our lives, including some of the Numbers explained from Chapter 3 onward. When a Master Number crops up in a significant date, for example 11 September or 9/11, it becomes a pivotal point of reference to show us where we've been, what we're doing and calling us to service. Master Number energies provide us with opportunities to awaken group consciousness through love and service.

We can take a look around us and notice how Master Numbers are influencing life both in history and right now, and learn from them. These energies are awe-inspiring if we can grasp their true potential. They act like guides for our highest good.

What qualities are associated with particular Master Numbers?

Master Number 11

This energy is fiery and wilful. It helps to purify the heart and the mind, and to cleanse out dross from old experiences. It's like being in love, with the whole of the universe channelling through at the speed of light. The head is spinning, the heart is racing, the temperature is soaring, and consciousness is rising. We can use Master Number 11 to raise hopes and expectations, and even when there are disappointments we still hold in mind the positive ideal. Co-dependency, fear and intense emotions are brought into balance, enhancing intuition, clarity and wisdom.

Master Number 22

This energy is solid and strategic and carries deep soul sensitivity. It helps us to return to the womb of life and connect with the original blueprint. It impresses upon humanity a need for thoughtful and careful planning. It encourages co-operation, bridge-building, sharing, receptivity and love in order to build a new world together.

Master Number 33

This creative and compassionate energy is totally available to be used for the greater good. Life is service, and pure sacrifice is the way humanity learns to let go of self-gratification and self-importance. Master Number 33 provides us with intense experiences to open the heart. Although it also carries the qualities of resentment, emotional martyrdom, obsession and bitterness, soul allows these energies to melt away in the light of compassion, generosity and acceptance of the divine.

Master Number 44

This energy is like lightning; it destroys, reconstructs and energizes all at once. It helps humanity to wake up to its responsibilities. It teaches us to accept direction from others while being true to ourselves. It asks us to endure life and carry on with the work. This master energy is often present during times of great hardship or the darkest nights of the soul. We're re-evaluating, cutting ties with the past and gaining strength from within.

Master Number 55

This energy is like being in the eye of a hurricane. We experience stillness within our soul because we're connected with the pure light of spirit and we remain largely unaffected by the torrent of change going on around us. Master energy 55 appears when it's time to rip away old patterns, to bring soul back to life, and to break through if there has been a breakdown (in communication). It brings freedom and its restless energy keeps us on our toes. The risk of obsessive control, mental fragility and addictions teach us to turn inward to cleanse emotional misconceptions and to apply common sense. Courageous leadership moves us forward together.

Master Number 66

This energy feels complete, yet it is open and welcoming. The world is full of many colourful cultures and our common thread is love. Giving love and service is not a duty – it's an intrinsic part of humanity's energetic make-up. We may harbour guilt or shame (personally or collectively on behalf of our family or community) or blame others for our misfortunes. We are nature so we are imperfect. This master energy can teach us to reflect, recognize and let go of the past. If we interfere in the process of life, it will take us longer to reach new levels of wholeness and harmony.

Master Number 77

This energy is stirring and all-pervasive. It can tumble down walls and barriers to create a fast network connection between mind, soul and nature. It teaches us to question everything about life and the universe and then to distribute the information to others. This master energy strips away identity and renders everything back to pure energy to provide continuity of life.

Master Number 88

This energy is fluid yet holds us upright, allowing our inner spiritual spine to act as a transmitter for the light. In quiet inner reflection we can see a mirror of society within ourselves and we cut ties with the past because great lessons have been learned. This master energy is waking us up to our deepest soul potential and aligning us to the higher spiritual will. It tests and mocks us (in case we are too serious). We are often hard on ourselves, stubborn, and can sabotage life, but this teaches us to be flexible.

Master Number 99

This energy is all-encompassing. If we feel overwhelmed it is the energy of soul overshadowing our daily existence. This energy feels vague and at other times it's so tangible it's as if we can reach out and touch it. Master Number 99 represents pure soul and wisdom. It contains all the other Master Numbers within it, so it is a very potent guide for humanity. It provides us with tough love, hope, forgiveness and selfless service. This energy is impossible to pin down because it's always adapting like a chameleon to its environment. It no longer needs to be attached to an identity, no longer focuses on personal desires or needs, so fits in with everything and everyone; soul is within us and all is well.

What next?

Now that you've been shown how to work out some of the most important Numbers in your life, you may find it useful to bring them together in a Birth Chart (see example opposite) to get an overall feel for how your Numerological energies are blending and what this could mean in your life.

You can list all the key information in any order you want. You may want to include other names and numbers that have special significance in your life too, such as your graduation day, your wedding day, your married name and so on. Your Birth Chart can be as short or long as you want.

Once you've compiled your chosen information, take a break from it. When you come back to it, start gazing at it without thinking of anything in particular. Soon you are likely to get some strong impressions. You may well be drawn toward some specific numbers, so start there – and use the relevant Number interpretations within this book to help you to feel into your intuition. Feel free to make notes beside the Numbers or to write a summary of the insights that you find most useful.

When this approach is taken to Diana's chart, the Numbers show she was kind and empathetic but also stubborn and wilful – slowly learning to trust life and communicate her truth.

CASESTUDY PRINCESS DIANA BIRTH CHART

Birth names	Diana Frances Spencer	Soul Vibration No. 9
		Name No. 4
		Karmic Key Nos. 2, 8
First name	Diana	Goal No. 2
Middle name	Frances	Support Name No. 3
Family name	Spencer	Family Name No. 8
Date of birth	1.7.1961	Personality No. 1
		Life Purpose No. 7
Married name	Her Royal Highness the Princess of Wales	3
Wedding day	29.7.1981	Master No. 55
Divorce date	28.8.1996	7
Name after divorce	Diana, Princess of Wales	6
Date of death	31.8.1997	Personal Year No. 7
		General Date No. 11
		Day No. 4

So now it's over to you to start creating charts of your own, both for yourself and others. I hope that it enriches your life with as much joy and insight as it has mine.

Further reading

By Sonia Ducie:

Choose the Perfect Baby Name (Watkins)

The Complete Illustrated Guide to Numerology (Element)

Do It Yourself Numerology: How to Unlock the Secrets of Your Personality with Numbers (Element/Watkins)

First Directions Numerology (Thorsons)

The Lucky Numbers Oracle (Thorsons)

Numerology Gem (Collins)

Numerology: Your Love and Relationship Guide (Element)

Numerology: Your Personal Guide to Life (Element/Watkins)

Power Pendants in a Box: Wear Your Lucky Numbers Every Day (Connections)

The Principles of Numerology (Thorsons)

Sonia Ducie's Numerology Secrets (Thorsons)

By Claudine Aegerter:

The Spirit of the Tarot: Numbers as Initiators of the Major Arcana (Aeon Books)

Professional organizations

The Association Internationale de Numerologues (AIN) and the Connaissance School of Numerology (CSN) were formed in 1993 in the UK by Claudine Aegerter. She is Principal of the Connaissance School. Sonia became the first Secretary of AIN when it was formed along with CSN in 1993, and she is currently a Council Member.

For Numerology readings, international courses, workshops, business seminars and professional training, visit www.numerologyworld.org.

Or write to AIN, 8 Melbourn Street, Royston, SG8 7BZ, UK

ABOUT THE AUTHOR

SONIA DUCIE

Sonia Ducie, Dip. CSN. AIN, is a teacher with the Connaissance School of Numerology, and best-selling author of 12 Numerology books translated into 14 languages. She has been giving readings for more than 23 years in the areas of business, relationships and compatibility; health & lifestyle; baby names; name-changing; careers; soul growth; and personal transformation. Sonia offers professional training in Esoteric Numerology, Esoteric Tarot and Business. Her mission is to help raise collective consciousness. She intends to inspire others to be successful in all areas of their lives by tapping into the creative power of Numerology.

www.Twitter.com/SoniaDucie

ABOUT THE SERIES

We hope you've enjoyed reading this book.
If you'd like to find out more about other therapies, practices
and phenomena that you've heard of and been curious about,
then do take a look at the other titles in our thought-provoking
#WHATIS series by visiting www.whatisseries.com

#WHATIS

The growing list of dynamic books in this series will allow
you to explore a wide range of life-enhancing topics – sharing
the history, wisdom and science of each subject, as well as
its far-reaching practical applications and benefits. With each guide
written by a practising expert in the field, this new series challenges
preconceptions, demystifies the subjects in hand and encourages
you to find new ways to lead a more fulfilled, meaningful and
contented life.

OTHER TITLES IN THE **#WHATIS** SERIES:

What is a Near-Death Experience? by Dr Penny Sartori
What is Sound Healing? by Lyz Cooper
What is Hypnosis? by Tom Fortes Mayer
What is Post-Traumatic Growth? by Miriam Akhtar
What is Mindfulness? by Dr Tamara Russell

WATKINS

Sharing Wisdom Since
1893

The story of Watkins dates back to 1893, when the scholar of esotericism John Watkins founded a bookshop, inspired by the lament of his friend and teacher Madame Blavatsky that there was nowhere in London to buy books on mysticism, occultism or metaphysics. That moment marked the birth of Watkins, soon to become the home of many of the leading lights of spiritual literature, including Carl Jung, Rudolf Steiner, Alice Bailey and Chögyam Trungpa.

Today, the passion at Watkins Publishing for vigorous questioning is still resolute. Our wide-ranging and stimulating list reflects the development of spiritual thinking and new science over the past 120 years. We remain at the cutting edge, committed to publishing books that change lives.

DISCOVER MORE . . .

Read our blog

Watch and listen to
our authors in action

Sign up to
our mailing list

JOIN IN THE CONVERSATION

 WatkinsPublishing   @watkinswisdom

 watkinsbooks   watkinswisdom   watkins-media

Our books celebrate conscious, passionate, wise and happy living.
Be part of the community by visiting

www.watkinspublishing.com